SPORTSWIT

SPORTSWIT

Researched and Compiled by

Lee Green

1817

HARPER & ROW, PUBLISHERS, New York

Cambridge, Philadelphia, San Francisco,
London, Mexico City, São Paulo, Sydney

SPORTSWIT. Copyright © 1984 by Lee Green. All rights reserved. Printed in the United States of America. No part of this book may be used or reproduced in any manner whatsoever without written permission except in the case of brief quotations embodied in critical articles and reviews. For information address Harper & Row, Publishers, Inc., 10 East 53rd Street, New York, N.Y. 10022. Published simultaneously in Canada by Fitzhenry & Whiteside Limited, Toronto.

FIRST EDITION

Designer: C. Linda Dingler

Library of Congress Cataloging in Publication Data
Main entry under title:

Sportswit.

   Includes index.
   1. Sports—Quotations, maxims, etc.   I. Green, Lee.
GV706.8.S68   1984   796   83-48840
ISBN 0-06-015272-9   84 85 86 87 88 10 9 8 7 6 5 4 3 2 1
ISBN 0-06-091133-6 (pbk.) 84 85 86 87 88 10 9 8 7 6 5 4 3 2 1

Contents

Foreword

Kleber Cantrell isn't much of a baseball fan. It is May, 1950. Ted Williams is ripping American League pitching with vengeance befitting a man who, for want of a fraction of a percentage point in his batting average last season, failed to become the only player in major league history to win three triple crowns. But Cantrell, as fabricated by the late Thomas Thompson in his 1982 novel, *Celebrity,* has only a modest interest in the Red Sox slugger, an interest confined to "the covetous feeling that a man could play a child's game, make a quarter of a million a year, and have every public utterance and gesture committed to type and ink."

To be sure, Williams was better at the child's game than he was at public utterances. Not that he was reticent, but he was no poet. We remember almost nothing of what he said. What we remember is that in 1941 he batted over .400, and no major leaguer has done it since.

But I'm with Cantrell. Regardless of the merit, or lack thereof, of anything Williams ever uttered, it is astonishing how assiduously his words were monitored and committed to print. Not just the utterances of Williams, but those of sports personalities everywhere.

Some athletes are better suited to celebrity than others. Remembering his early unworldliness, Joe DiMaggio once revealed, "I can remember a reporter asking for a quote, and I didn't know what a quote was. I thought it was some kind of soft drink."

Today, with the ubiquity of television and radio reporters and the sheer numbers of print journalists, almost nothing is lost for posterity. We know what Lee Trevino says on the 15th tee at Pebble Beach; what Tommy Lasorda says between mouthfuls of linguini; and what Lou Holtz, God love him, says all the time. With the possible exception of heads of state, sports figures are the most closely monitored mammals in existence. But even heads of state don't have to submit to the indignity of accounting for themselves to reporters while peeling off their underwear after a day's work.

Our attentions have proved warranted. The sporting realm has been a fertile bastion for the clever rejoinder, the wry observation, the poignant phrase, the apt one-liner, the inane comment. It is inconceivable that such notable ripostes and witticisms could be derived from, say, auto mechanics, or doctors, or computer-software salesmen. Even politicians, with their practiced charisma and their perennial forum, don't compare favorably. Perhaps it is easier to be daft or glib about a missed field goal than about toxic waste dump sites.

Lest I sell politicians short, however, I hasten to add that history shows they do occasionally utter something worth repeating. Several politicians have found their way into this book, including United States Presidents Reagan, Carter, Ford, Nixon, Lyndon Johnson, Kennedy, Eisenhower, Hoover, Coolidge, Harding, Wilson and Teddy Roosevelt. There's nothing like sports to bring out the best in a person.

Sooner or later, everyone has something to say about sports, even if, as was the case with playwright Lillian Hellman, it is that they don't like them. "Mr. Dashiell Hammett spoiled me of all sports," she once lamented. "He was such a sports fan—a sports fiend, I should say—that he drove me crazy."

Journalist Sally Quinn shares the sentiment, at least where football is concerned. "The football season is like pain," she proclaims. "You forget how terrible it is until it seizes you again."

H. L. Mencken goes Hellman and Quinn one better, having once allowed, "I hate all sports as rabidly as a person who likes sports hates common sense." Mencken apparently took leave of his own common sense long enough to make that remark.

Sportswit is remarkably eclectic. I've mentioned the presidents. Also represented are such disparate individuals from outside the sports milieu as Johnny Carson, Rodney Dangerfield, David Brenner, Albert Einstein, Hugo Black, Oscar Wilde, Dean Martin, Tony Curtis, James Michener, John Updike, Art Buchwald, Abbie Hoffman, George Bernard Shaw, John Cheever, Howard K. Smith, Edward Kennedy, Bob Hope, Will Rogers, Pierre Trudeau, Erma Bombeck, William Saroyan, E.B. White, Elliott Gould, Tip O'Neill, Henry Ford, Henry Thoreau, Connie Stevens . . . and a confessed strangler named Richard T. Cooper who, in his final words before going to California's gas chamber in 1960, expressed heartfelt disenchantment with his favorite baseball team. "I'm very unhappy about the Giants," Cooper complained. "I didn't think Bill Rigney knew very much, but I don't think Tom Sheehan knows anything at all." Cooper was right. Rigney had the Giants in second place, but when Sheehan replaced him as manager, the club tumbled to fifth. Quite a fan, Cooper.

If there is a fan for all seasons, it is writer and pro athlete manqué George Plimpton, who once posited an interesting theory. He hypothesized that there exists an inverse correlation between the size of a ball and the quality of writing about the sport in which the ball is used. "There are superb books about golf," Plimpton explained, "very good books about baseball, not very many good books about football and very few good books about basketball. There are no good books about beach balls."

Intrigued, I tested Plimpton's theory while researching *Sportswit* and found it to be reasonably valid. What's more, I began to detect a similar relationship between ball size and the prevalence of good quotes about a sport. To wit, plenty of superb quotes relative to golf and baseball, fewer about basketball, and so forth. My corollary to the Plimpton Ball Theory was deflated, however, when I unearthed an abundance of worthy quotations about football, which utilizes a rather largish ball, and a striking disparity in the number of good quotes about baseball and tennis, which use balls roughly equal in size. I must admit, though, I found no quotes about beach balls—except Plimpton's.

However, I did find an interesting quote by Garp, as in *The World According to. . . .* "I do not care for balls," admitted John Irving's alter ego in the 1978 best-seller. "The ball stands between the athlete and his exercise. So do hockey pucks and badminton birdies—and skates, like skis, intrude between the body and the ground. And when one further removes one's body from the contest by an extension device—such as a racket, a bat, or a stick—all purity of movement, strength, and focus is lost."

Fortunately, not everyone feels the way Garp does, otherwise *Sportswit* would reflect an inordinate sum of rhetoric about wrestling. As it is, little of note has been said or written on the subject.

I could continue with the usual pap—a few words about the sports ethic, a line or two about sports being life in microcosm, at least a paragraph about the labors that have attended this volume. But you've heard it all before. Besides, I hold the firm belief that few readers bother to wade to the end of a foreword. However, to those who have gotten this far, I think your chances of appreciating *Sportswit* are quite good —unless you're predisposed toward quotes about wrestling. Or beach balls.

Lee Green

Ventura, California

About This Book

Furnishing appropriate identifications for authors of quotations in a book like this is perplexing, because the sporting world is in constant flux with its ceaseless hirings, firings, graduations, trades, drafts, retirements, franchise relocations and the like. Team affiliations tend to change more quickly than a reasonably voluble fan can blurt "Steinbrenner." There's "Billy Martin, New York Yankees manager" and "Billy Martin, Oakland A's manager"; "Bum Phillips, Houston Oilers coach" and "Bum Phillips, New Orleans Saints coach"; "Pete Rose, Cincinnati Reds outfielder" and "Pete Rose, Philadelphia Phillies first baseman."

The solution chosen for *Sportswit* was to identify each author by his affiliation at the time the quote was rendered. If the affiliation could not be ascertained because the date of the quote is uncertain, the identification has been generalized (e.g., "Billy Martin, major league manager"). The term "former" is used to denote authors who were retired when the relevant quote was rendered. In some cases, famous athletes who were associated with several teams and/or were quoted in retirement are identified as Hall of Fame members (e.g., "Ralph Kiner, Hall of Fame outfielder").

When a date is important to the context of a quote, it is provided. When a quote has been traced to more than one author, it is listed under the person most likely to have originated it; other attributions follow in parentheses. When two or more quotations are nearly identical, they are grouped with the most likely originator listed first.

When the author of a quote is better known by his nickname than his real name, as is frequently the case with sports figures, he is listed by his nickname (e.g., Bear Bryant, Red Smith, Babe Ruth, Digger Phelps). Nicknames of lesser-known individuals are in quotes (e.g., David "Smokey" Gaines), as are those commonly used in conjunction with a person's given name (e.g., Ed "Too Tall" Jones).

The Classics category merits special attention. This section consists of the best-known remarks, lyrics, verses and dialogues ever to evolve from the world of sport. Many of the lines identified as "classics" have been quoted and misquoted so frequently through the years that they've taken on lives of their own, gradually separating themselves from their derivations by myth and embellishment until we no longer remember who originated them or why. *Sportswit* offers some clarifications, though some answers are elusive. There's no telling, for instance, why a remark like Joe Jacobs' "I shoulda stood in bed" has enjoyed such robust immortality.

For whatever pains have been taken to insure that *Sportswit* contains the best sports quotes ever to come down the pike, undoubtedly some have escaped the author's attention. Additions and corrections may be addressed to Lee Green in care of Harper & Row, 10 East 53rd Street, New York, NY 10022.

SPORTSWIT

Academics

AL MCGUIRE
Marquette basketball coach-turned-sportscaster:

"I think everyone should go to college and get a degree and then spend six months as a bartender and six months as a cab driver. Then they would really be educated."

ALEX KARRAS
Detroit Lions defensive lineman:

"I never graduated from Iowa. I was only there for two terms —Truman's and Eisenhower's."

DR. GEORGE L. CROSS
Oklahoma University president:

"We're trying to build a university our football team can be proud of."

BEAR BRYANT
Alabama football coach, justifying the role of athletics at the university:

"It's kind of hard to rally 'round a math class."

ART BUCHWALD
humorist:

"Although I never played football, I made many contributions. I went to the University of Southern California in the late 1940s and took the English exams for all the Trojan linemen."

REV. THEODORE HESBURGH
Notre Dame University president, urging greater emphasis on academics for the school's athletes:

"A decade after graduation, almost everyone will have forgotten when and where and what they played. But every time they speak, everyone will know whether they are educated."

T. S. ELIOT
poet and critic, in the late 1930s:

"College football is becoming so complicated, players find it a recreation to go to classes."

GATES BROWN
major league outfielder, recalling high school:

"I took a little English, a little math, some science, a few hubcaps and some wheel covers."

DOUG WEAVER
Kansas State football coach, after being hanged in effigy on campus:

"I'm glad it happened in front of the library. I've always emphasized scholarship."

PAT MCINALLY
Cincinnati Bengals punter and holder of an art history degree from Harvard, on whether his major helped prepare him for a career in the NFL:

"Well, we do have a draw play here."

JAMES TAYLOR
College of Southern Idaho president, reacting to outcries against his dropping three sports and five coaches to solve a financial crisis:

"I should have dropped the math and English departments and study hall. Then no one would have known about it."

SHELBY METCALF
Texas A & M basketball coach, to a player who received four F's and a D:

"Son, looks to me like you're spending too much time on one subject."

DAVID "SMOKEY" GAINES
San Diego State basketball coach:

"I believe in higher education. You know, 6–8, 6–9, 6–10. . . ."

MARVIN BARNES
Boston Celtics forward, on why he earned so many college credits while in prison:

"There was no place I could go to cut classes."

DEWEY SELMON
Tampa Bay Buccaneers linebacker, on his pursuit of a Ph.D. in philosophy:

"Philosophy is just a hobby. You can't open up a philosophy factory."

ABE LEMONS
Texas basketball coach, recalling when two of his players at Oklahoma City University enrolled in a basket-weaving class:

"The only problem was that the instructor graded on the curve and there were twenty-four Indians in the class. Both my guys flunked."

JOHNNY WALKER
Baltimore disc jockey:

"The University of Maryland football team members all make straight A's. Their B's are a little crooked."

Age

SATCHEL PAIGE
Hall of Fame pitcher:

"Age is a question of mind over matter. If you don't mind, it doesn't matter."

HUGO BLACK
U.S. Supreme Court justice:

"When I was 40, my doctor advised me that a man in his forties shouldn't play tennis. I heeded his advice carefully and could hardly wait until I reached 50 to start again."

CASEY STENGEL
major league manager:

"Old-timers weekends and airplane landings are alike. If you can walk away from them, they're successful."

CASEY STENGEL
New York Yankees manager, when the club didn't renew his contract after the Yankees lost the 1960 World Series to the Pittsburgh Pirates:

"I'll never make the mistake again of being 70 years old."

JOE DIMAGGIO
Hall of Fame outfielder, on being designated baseball's "greatest living player" at age 66:

"At my age, I'm just happy to be named the greatest living anything."

JOHN F. KENNEDY
thirty-fifth President of the United States, at age 45, to 42-year-old St. Louis Cardinals first baseman Stan Musial at the 1962 All-Star game:

"A couple of years ago they told me I was too young to be President and you were too old to be playing baseball. But we fooled them."

RONALD REAGAN
fortieth President of the United States, to Gaylord Perry shortly before the 43-year-old pitcher won his three-hundredth major league game:

"I just know that it's an ugly rumor that you and I are the only two people left alive who saw Abner Doubleday throw the first pitch out."

4

DR. PHOG ALLEN
former Kansas basketball coach, at age 79:

"You're not old until it takes you longer to rest up than it does to get tired."

FRANKLIN P. ADAMS
humorist:

"Middle age occurs when you are too young to take up golf and too old to rush up to the net."

CHRIS DUNDEE
boxing promoter:

"Middle age is when you start for home about the same time you used to start for something else."

VIN SCULLY
sportscaster:

"It's a mere moment in a man's life between an All-Star game and an old-timers game."

BILL LEE
major league pitcher:

"If I were a Tibetan priest and ate everything perfect, maybe I'd live to be 105. The way I'm going now, I'll probably only make it to 102. I'll give away three years to beer."

HORATIO LURO
80-year-old horse trainer, revealing his prescription for longevity:

"Swim, dance a little, go to Paris every August and live within walking distance of two hospitals."

HERMAN "JACKRABBIT" SMITH-JOHANNSEN
103-year-old Canadian cross-country skier, revealing his prescription for longevity:

"Stay busy, get plenty of exercise and don't drink too much. Then again, don't drink too little."

GARY HAMMOND
Southern Methodist University quarterback, after his final college game:

"You start out in college worrying about growing up, and when you finish you're worrying about growing old."

BRANCH RICKEY
major league baseball executive, on the stages of senility:

"First you forget names; then you forget faces; then you forget to zip up your fly; and then you forget to unzip your fly."

GEORGE MACINTYRE
Vanderbilt football coach, surveying a roster that included 26 freshmen and 25 sophomores:

"Our biggest concern this season will be diaper rash."

TONY CURTIS
actor, on why he quit smoking:

"I like to think of it in simple terms. Smoking shortens your life by eight years. I love watching pro football on television. If I smoke, I'll miss 350 games."

EARLY WYNN
Hall of Fame pitcher:

"First thing I do when I wake up in the morning is breathe on a mirror and hope it fogs."

TOMMY LASORDA
Los Angeles Dodgers manager, as a 37-year-old veteran ran past the dugout:

"There goes Rick Monday. He and Manny Mota are so old they were waiters at The Last Supper."

STAN WILLIAMS
New York Yankees coach, on veteran outfielder Oscar Gamble:

"Oscar is so old that when he broke into the majors he was still a Negro."

DOUG DIEKEN
Cleveland Browns offensive lineman, on Houston Oilers veteran defensive end Elvin Bethea:

"Elvin is so old he had to use a jumper cable to get started last year."

CAL HUBBARD
former major league umpire:

"If I'd known I was going to grow this old, I'd have taken better care of myself."

CASEY STENGEL
former New York Yankees manager, at age 71:

"Most people are dead at my age—and you could look it up."

SATCHEL PAIGE
Hall of Fame pitcher:

"How old would you be if you didn't know how old you was?"

Alumni

LOU HOLTZ
Arkansas football coach:

"The only thing universal about alumni is that they end every season with 'but.' Like, 'We had a good season, but . . .' "

PHIL CUTCHIN
former Oklahoma State football coach, on why he quit to become a cattle rancher:

"Cattle have no alumni."

ANONYMOUS ALUMNUS
in a telegram to Michigan State football coach Duffy Daugherty shortly before a big game:

"Remember, Coach, we're all behind you—win or tie."

Anecdotes

MARTY SPRINGSTEAD

baseball umpire, will never forget his first major league game, a 1965 contest at Washington. When huge Frank Howard of the Senators made his first appearance at the plate, Springstead called a knee-high pitch a strike.

Springstead: "Howard turned around and hollered, 'Get something straight, buster. I don't know where you came from or what you're doing in the major leagues, but they don't call a strike on me with that pitch. Understand?' "

The next pitch was in the same spot, and Springstead yelled, "Two!"

Howard (irate): "Two what?"

Springstead: "Too low, Frank. It was much too low."

BOB UECKER

baseball announcer, was a notoriously weak hitter when he played in the major leagues.

Uecker: "I remember one time I'm batting against the Dodgers in Milwaukee. They lead, two–one, it's the bottom of the ninth, bases loaded, two out and the pitcher has a full count on me.

"I look over to the Dodger dugout and they're all in street clothes."

MUHAMMAD ALI

heavyweight boxing champion, lost a battle of wits with a stewardess on an Eastern Airlines flight.

Stewardess: "Mr. Ali, please fasten your seat belt."

Ali: "Superman don't need no seat belt."

Stewardess: "Superman don't need no airplane, either."

TOMMY BOLT

professional golfer, earned the nickname Terrible Tommy because of his temper on the golf course, which frequently induced him to abuse his clubs. Once he was about 125 yards from a green and his caddie recommended a two-iron.

Bolt: "A two-iron?"
Caddie: "Tommy, it's the only one left in your bag."

POTTER STEWART
U.S. Supreme Court justice, was bent on staying abreast of a Cincinnati Reds–N.Y. Mets National League playoff game in 1973, so he asked his clerks to send batter-by-batter bulletins to the bench where he was hearing oral arguments. One such update informed him:

"Kranepool flies to right. Agnew resigns."

RICK MONDAY
Los Angeles Dodgers outfielder, was close friends in high school with a fellow named Steve Sunday and another named George Washington.

Monday: "One night we were all out together and the police stopped us for running a red light. When they asked our names, our driver said, 'I'm Steve Sunday'; and then I said, 'I'm Rick Monday'; and then the cop with the flashlight pointed it at the other guy, saying, 'And I suppose you're George Washington?' When George nodded yes, I think they would have locked us up if he hadn't pulled out his ID and proved it."

JACK DALY
football official in Maine, tells of an insecure wife questioning her laconic husband on what would happen if she died.

Wife: "I suppose you already have your eye on some pretty young thing to succeed me."
Husband: "Maybe."
Wife: "And I suppose you would even have her share our bedroom and bed."
Husband: "Maybe."
Wife: "And I suppose you would even let her use my golf clubs."
Husband: "Nope. She's left-handed."

LARRY GUEST
sportswriter, chronicled an exchange between major league baseball owners' representative Ray Grebey and Minnesota Twins player representative Mike Marshall during 1980 contract negotiations:

"When Grebey made what Marshall considered a ludicrous point, the pitcher with the Ph.D. (in exercise physiology) reached into his advanced educational background and shouted across the table, 'Bullbleep!' Or something very close to bullbleep.

"Momentarily taken aback, Grebey regrouped, summoned his years of experience in rational labor debate and returned serve. 'Bullbleep!' he shouted.

" 'Bullbleep!' Marshall echoed.

"Before this warm dialogue ended—when Grebey stalked angrily out of the room—he and Marshall reportedly had fired off six consecutive bullbleeps, believed to be a major league record."

SAM SNEAD
professional golfer, was playing his third shot on the 16th at Firestone Country Club and asked his caddie what club to use.

Caddie: "Well, yesterday I caddied for Jay Hebert and he hit an 8-iron."
Snead proceeded to hit an 8-iron, only to see his ball disappear into the lake in front of the green.
Snead: "Do you mean to tell me Hebert hit an 8 here?"
Caddie: "Yes sir, he did."
Snead: "Where'd he hit it?"
Caddie: "Oh, Mr. Hebert hit it into the lake too."

FRESCO THOMPSON
Philadelphia Phillies captain, delivered a lineup card to umpire Bill Klem with the following notation in the ninth spot:

"Willoughby and others."

BABE RUTH
New York Yankees outfielder, suffered the humiliation of having the great Walter Johnson of the Washington Senators throw three straight fastballs past him. When he asked the umpire if he had seen any of the pitches, the ump said no.

Ruth: "Neither did I, but that last one sounded kinda high to me."

BOB UECKER
major league catcher-turned-broadcaster, once reviewed his career highlights with Johnny Carson on the *Tonight* show.

Uecker: "I made a major contribution to the Cardinals' pennant drive in '64—I came down with hepatitis."
Carson: "How'd you catch it?"
Uecker: "The trainer injected me with it."

FRANK HOWARD
Los Angeles Dodgers outfielder, had reached first base on a walk. The prearranged sign for the hit-and-run was the mention of the baserunner's last name, so first-base coach Pete Reiser said, "Okay, Howard, on your toes. *Howard,* be ready for anything." Howard called time and walked over to Reiser.

"Pete, we're good friends. Call me Frank."

JOE DINEEN
sportswriter, tells of the golfer who had problems on the first hole:

"He sliced his ball into a thicket of bushes, then went into a sand trap, then shanked one across the highway, then back into some heavy woods. Undaunted, he went to find his ball, but it was irretrievably lost.

" 'Why don't you forget it and drop another one?' asked his playing companion.

" 'I can't,' the undaunted one replied. 'It's my lucky ball.' "

JERRY GUIBOR
sportswriter, wanted to discreetly telephone an Arizona State football player for an interview, so he called the Sun Devils' 73-year-old equipment manager Chester Kropp.

Guibor: "Chester, do you happen to have Gary Bouck's number?"
Kropp: "Just a minute."
Guibor waited for a seeming eternity before Kropp returned to the phone.
Kropp: "Sixty-five."

PAUL HORNUNG
Notre Dame quarterback, was caught snuffing out a cigarette by Notre Dame coach Frank Leahy.

Leahy: "Do you see what I see near your shoe, Paul?"
Hornung: "Yeah, coach, I see. But you take it. You saw it first."

LOU HOLTZ
Arkansas football coach, had a standing offer to visit Jackie Sherrill's Pennsylvania home when Sherrill coached at Pitt.

Holtz: "Jackie once told me to come by for a visit when I was in the area. I did just that, one morning about three. Not sure that I was at the right address, I honked the horn, and Mrs. Sherrill appeared at the front door. I said, 'Is this where Jackie Sherrill lives?' She said, 'Yeah, just bring him in and lay him down in the hall like everybody else does.' "

MICKEY MCDERMOTT
New York Yankees pitcher, was famed for his after-hours escapades. He once tried to sneak into his hotel room at 4:00 A.M. by taking the freight elevator. When the elevator door opened, the pitcher was greeted by Yankees manager Casey Stengel.

Stengel: "Drunk again."
McDermott, grinning impishly: "Me too."

LEFTY GOMEZ
major league pitcher, was due to bat against hard-throwing and erratic Bob Feller. Daylight was on the wane, so Gomez produced a book of matches at the plate and struck one.

Home plate umpire Bill Summers: "What's the matter with you, Gomez? You know you can see Feller perfectly well."

Gomez: "Yeah, I just want to be sure he sees me."

DAFFY DEAN
St. Louis Cardinals pitcher, was swigging a bottle of soda pop just as the train he and his teammates were riding entered a long tunnel. Sportswriter Grantland Rice overheard this exchange between Daffy and his brother Dizzy:

Daffy: "Diz, you tried any of this stuff?"

Dizzy: "Just fixin' to. Why?"

Daffy: "Don't! I did, and I've gone plumb blind."

JACK BALDSCHUN
former Philadelphia Phillies pitcher, recalled a game in Houston, in the days before the Astrodome, when Phillies manager Gene Mauch exploded because players were complaining about the scorching heat.

"Gene went into this big tirade: 'I'm sick of you guys griping about the climate. The other guys have to play in it too. Next guy who complains about the heat gets fined a hundred bucks.'

"The next inning, Johnny Callison comes back from the outfield, flops down on the bench and says, 'God, is it hot out there.' Just then he remembers what Mauch said. So, real quick, Johnny says, 'Good 'n hot, just the way I like it.' "

JOHN DREW
Atlanta Hawks forward, had the following exchange with a front-office secretary who was obtaining data for an insurance form:

Secretary: "What's your birth date, John?"

Drew: "September 30."

Secretary: "What year?"

Drew: "Every year."

CHI CHI RODRIGUEZ
professional golfer, tells of driving conditions in his native Puerto Rico:

"A man motoring in Puerto Rico goes through a red light and his passenger asks why. He says because his brother does it. He goes through another red light, the passenger asks why, and he again says his brother does it. Then he comes to a green light, slams on the brakes and screeches to a stop. His passenger asks why, and he says, 'Because my brother might be coming.' "

JOE GARAGIOLA
baseball broadcaster, was a catcher for the St. Louis Cardinals and several other National League teams when Warren Spahn was a stand-

out pitcher for the Milwaukee Braves. Long after their careers had ended, the two players reminisced together.

Spahn: "I always loved to see Garagiola coming to bat. I owned him."

Garagiola: "Yeah, it used to embarrass me when you sent your limousine to the hotel for me and the guy would announce, 'Warren Spahn's car is here for Mr. Garagiola.' "

VINCE LOMBARDI

Green Bay Packers coach, had a marvelous sense of humor beneath his gruff exterior. Paul Hornung, who played for Lombardi, tells this story about the coach:

"One night, after a long, cold, difficult day, Lombardi came home late and tumbled into bed. 'God,' his wife said, 'your feet are cold.' And Lombardi answered, 'Around the house, dear, you may call me Vince.' "

JOE GILMARTIN

Phoenix sportswriter, called Oakland A's owner Charlie Finley for an interview, but every time he asked a question, Finley responded, "That's none of your damned business." Perplexed, Gilmartin offered one final innocuous question about a player.

Finley: "That's none of your damned business. I don't know what I'm doing talking to you, anyway. Phoenix? What's Phoenix to me? What's the circulation of your paper, anyway?"

Gilmartin: "That's none of your damned business."

TOM LANDRY

Dallas Cowboys coach, drove to the team's practice facility one rainy morning and found his parking space occupied by a car belonging to rookie linebacker Steve Kiner. Soaking wet, he entered the dressing room, looked squarely at Kiner and said:

"I admire a man with courage."

SCOTTY BYERS

Long Beach State cornerback, received a ferocious hit in a game against Southwest Louisiana, prompting coach Dave Currey to rush to his side to check his condition.

Currey: "What's your name?"
Byers: "Who wants to know?"

DICK WILLIAMS

Montreal Expos manager, in a game against the Phillies, ordered an intentional walk to Bake McBride with runners on second and third. Mike Schmidt then laced a single to win the game for the Phils. Afterward, Williams tried to defend his strategy.

Williams: "I don't care if Jesus Christ was coming up, I was going to walk McBride."

Reporter: "What if Babe Ruth was coming up?"

Williams [after a pause]: "I don't know about Babe Ruth."

DON LIDDLE

New York Giants relief pitcher, found himself in a tight spot in the opening game of the 1954 World Series. Manager Leo Durocher summoned him from the bullpen in the eighth inning, score tied, Cleveland with a pair of runners on base, one out and Vic Wertz at the plate.

Wertz blasted a drive some 460 feet to the deepest part of the Polo Grounds, only to have Giants center fielder Willie Mays turn his back on the plate and make a brilliant—and now famous—over-the-shoulder catch on a dead run.

Replaced by another reliever, Liddle walked to the dugout, laid down his glove and said:

"Well, I got *my* man."

JIM DURFEE

NFL official, had the rare distinction of always getting the final word with Chicago Bears owner/coach George Halas. Once, when Halas was riding him mercilessly, he began marching off a five-yard penalty.

Halas: "What's that for?"

Durfee: "Coaching from the sideline."

Halas: "Well, that just proves how dumb you are. That's 15 yards, not five."

Durfee: "Yeah, but the penalty for your kind of coaching is only five yards."

LOU GEHRIG

New York Yankees first baseman, was under contract to endorse Post Toasties cereal. Robert Ripley, on his live television program *Believe It or Not,* gave Gehrig his cue.

Ripley: "What do you have every morning, Lou?"

Gehrig: "A heaping bowlful of Wheaties!"

JACK KAISER

Philadelphia sportswriter, couldn't believe how long it took the final second to elapse in a game between the 76ers and the Portland Trail Blazers. With the clock seemingly frozen, Archie Clark of the 76ers dribbled left, dribbled right, faked right and finally put up a game-winning shot.

Kaiser (to Portland sportswriter Wayne Thompson): "Where's the timer, where's the timer? I want to see him. I've got to see him!"

Thompson: "He's gone. Besides, you can't interview him, anyway."

Kaiser: "I don't want to interview him. I just want him to time the rest of my life."

DIZZY DEAN

Hall of Fame pitcher who worked as a radio broadcaster following his retirement from baseball, was announcing a St. Louis Browns game when he noticed a commotion in the stands below the broadcast booth:

"I don't know what all the commotion down there is," he informed his listeners, "but it has somethin' to do with a fat lady."

A startled executive for the station who happened to be in the booth pulled Dean away from the mike and told him the fat lady happened to be the Queen of the Netherlands. After inquiring as to the whereabouts of the Netherlands, Dean leaned back over his mike and reported, "I've just been informed that the fat lady is the Queen of Holland."

Aphorisms

BRANCH RICKEY
major league baseball executive:

"Problems are the price you pay for progress."

BAT MASTERSON
sports editor:

"Everybody in life gets the same amount of ice. The rich get it in the summer and the poor in winter."
(Found in Masterson's typewriter following his fatal heart attack)

LOU HOLTZ
Arkansas football coach:

"Genius: It's 1 percent inspiration and 99 percent perspiration. No one has ever drowned in sweat."
(The first sentence of this quotation is commonly attributed to inventor Thomas Edison)

JOHN WOODEN
UCLA basketball coach:

"It's not so important who starts the game, but who finishes it."

BRANCH RICKEY
major league baseball executive:

"Prefer the errors of enthusiasm to the complacency of wisdom."

BUM PHILLIPS
Houston Oilers coach:

"An expert is an ordinary fella away from home."

FRED SHERO
New York Rangers coach and general manager:

"To avoid criticism, say nothing, do nothing, be nothing."

ANONYMOUS

"Winners never quit and quitters never win."
(Thought to have been inspired by Illinois football coach Bob Zuppke)

ANONYMOUS

"When the going gets tough, the tough get going."

CASEY STENGEL
major league manager:

"Most ball games are lost, not won."

MARK TWAIN
writer:

"It is the difference of opinion that makes horse races."

JOHN WOODEN
UCLA basketball coach:

"Be quick, but never hurry."

FRED SHERO
New York Rangers coach and general manager:

"Temptation rarely comes in working hours. It's in their leisure time that men are made or marred."

LOU HOLTZ
Arkansas football coach:

"You never get ahead of anyone as long as you try to get even with him."

FRED RUSSELL
sportswriter/editor:

"Nothing exceeds like excess."

LOU HOLTZ
Arkansas football coach:

"When all is said and done, as a rule, more is said than done."

YOGI BERRA
major league catcher/manager/coach:

"The game's not over till it's over."

LOU HOLTZ
Arkansas football coach:

"If you burn your neighbor's house down, it doesn't make your house look better."

Aspirations

GERALD R. FORD
thirty-eighth President of the United States:

"I've had a lifelong ambition to be a professional baseball player, but nobody would sign me."

(Ford was offered a pro football contract after winning MVP honors at Michigan in 1934, but chose to study law at Yale.)

A. BARTLETT GIAMATTI
Yale University president:

"All I ever wanted to be president of was the American League."

TED WILLIAMS
Boston Red Sox slugger:

"All I want out of life is that when I walk down the street, folks will say, 'There goes the greatest hitter who ever lived.' "

TED TURNER
Atlanta Hawks and Braves owner:

"One of my goals in life was to be surrounded by unpretentious, rich young men. Then I bought the Braves and I was surrounded by 25 of them."

DWIGHT D. EISENHOWER
thirty-fourth President of the United States:

"When I was a small boy in Kansas, a friend of mine and I went fishing, and as we sat there in the warmth of a summer afternoon on a riverbank, we talked about what we wanted to do when we grew up. I told him that I wanted to be a real major league baseball player, a genuine professional like Honus Wagner. My friend said that he'd like to be President of the United States. Neither of us got our wish."

GRAIG NETTLES
New York Yankees third baseman:

"When I was a little boy, I wanted to be a baseball player and join the circus. With the Yankees I've accomplished both."

JOHN SAYLES
writer:

"I never thought about being a writer as I grew up; a writer wasn't something to be. An outfielder was something to be. Most of what I know about style I learned from Roberto Clemente."

SHIRLEY MULDOWNEY
auto drag racer:

"I want to be the fastest woman in the world—in a manner of speaking."

LOU HOLTZ
Arkansas football coach:

"I really only ever wanted two things. First, I never really wanted to be rich. Second, I never really wanted to be poor."

Atheists

DWIGHT D. EISENHOWER
thirty-fourth President of the United States:

"An atheist is a guy who watches a Notre Dame–S.M.U. football game and doesn't care who wins."

WALLY BUTTS
Georgia athletic director:

"The definition of an atheist in Alabama is a person who doesn't believe in Bear Bryant."

Athletes

FINLEY PETER DUNNE
humorist, as represented by his fictional Irish saloon keeper/philosopher Mr. Dooley:

"In my younger days it was not considered respectable to be an athlete. An athlete was always a man that was not strong enough to work."

MIKE NEWLIN
New Jersey Nets guard:

"The problem with many athletes is they take themselves seriously and their sport lightly."

BRUCE JENNER
Olympic decathlon champion:

"An athlete has such a narrow view of life he does not know reality."

EMIL ZATOPEK
Czechoslovakian Olympic distance-running champion:

"Sportsmen are like children. They don't know anything about life. They know only to train and compete. They meet only other sportsmen."

Attire

JIM MURRAY
sportswriter, on Bear Bryant:

"The man has been a refugee from a steam iron for 40 years."

LEE CORSO
Indiana football coach, explaining his quiltlike sportscoat:

"It's my interview jacket. No matter what the colors of the school, they're in that coat."

BOB BORKOWSKI
assistant football coach at Ferris State College, asked why he showed up for a game in a black, pin-striped, vested suit:

"I wanted to look nice if we won, and if we lost this would be nice to be buried in."

GARY PLAYER
South African professional golfer, on why he wears black:

"I loved westerns, and the cowboys always looked good in black."

SANDY SANDERS
boot maker, on why then Houston Oilers coach Bum Phillips insisted on boots with pointed toes:

"You can't climb fences real fast with a rounded toe, and someday he's gonna be in a hell of a hurry to get out of the Astrodome."

JASON THOMPSON
Detroit Tigers first baseman, when manager Sparky Anderson announced a ban on jeans:

"There goes my wardrobe."

JERRY REUSS
Los Angeles Dodgers pitcher, after noticing a radio announcer dressed in a yellow shirt and red pants:

"Why don't you buy a green hat and hire out as a traffic signal?"

Autographs

CASEY STENGEL
major league manager:

"I love signing autographs. I'll sign anything but veal cutlets. My ball-point pen slips on veal cutlets."

BILL RUSSELL
former Boston Celtics center:

"In the autograph business, either the fans are prostrate and the stars are high-and-mighty, or vice versa. There's no such thing as an even keel, which is why the whole thing is phony."

WILLIE WILSON
Kansas City Royals outfielder, on why he refuses to sign autographs:

"When I was a little kid, teachers used to punish me by making me sign my name 100 times."

Auto Racing

RED SMITH
sportswriter:

"This is a sport?"

STIRLING MOSS
English race driver:

"To achieve anything in this game, you must be prepared to dabble on the boundary of disaster."

MARIO ANDRETTI
race driver:

"When somebody screws up in front of you at 200 miles per hour, man, school's out."

DARRELL WALTRIP
race driver:

"If the lion didn't bite the tamer every once in a while, it wouldn't be exciting."

STIRLING MOSS
English race driver:

"It is necessary to relax your muscles when you can. Relaxing your brain is fatal."

EDDIE SACHS
race driver:

"Your car moves faster than you can think."

JANET GUTHRIE
race driver, downplaying the importance of strength in her sport:

"You drive the car, you don't carry it."

WHITEY GERKEN
race driver, on his heroic act of stopping his car during a race to pull an unconscious opponent from his overturned racer:

"Aw, why not? I wasn't running well anyway."

25

A. J. FOYT
race driver:

"I feel safer on a racetrack with the traffic going in the same direction and good drivers behind the wheels than I do on Houston expressways."

JIM MURRAY
sportswriter, on the Indianapolis 500:

"It's not so much a sporting event as a deathwatch. They hold it, fittingly, on Memorial Day."

GEORGE ROBSON
race driver, after winning the 1946 Indianapolis 500:

"All I had to do was keep turning left."

JACKIE STEWART
English race driver:

"In my sport, the quick are too often listed among the dead."

Baseball

BILL VEECK
major league owner:

"Baseball is almost the only orderly thing in a very unorderly world. If you get three strikes, even the best lawyer in the world can't get you off."

JIM MURRAY
sportswriter:

"Baseball is a game where a curve is an optical illusion, a screwball can be a pitch or a person, stealing is legal and you can spit anywhere you like except in the umpire's eye or on the ball."

WES WESTRUM
San Francisco Giants coach:

"It's like church. Many attend, but few understand."

WILLIAM SAROYAN
writer:

"Baseball is caring. Player and fan alike must care, or there's no game, there's no pennant race and no World Series. And for all any of us know, there might soon be no nation at all."

JIM MURRAY
sportswriter:

"The charm of baseball is that, dull as it may be on the field, it is endlessly fascinating as a rehash."

BRUCE CATTON
writer/historian:

"Say this much for big league baseball—it is beyond any question the greatest conversation piece ever invented in America."

JACQUES BARZUN
writer/historian:

"Whoever would understand the heart and mind of America had better learn baseball."

ALBERT EINSTEIN
physicist, to major league catcher Moe Berg after suggesting that he teach Berg mathematics and Berg teach him baseball:

"But I'm sure you'd learn mathematics faster than I'd learn baseball."

RICHARD T. COOPER
confessed strangler, disapproving of his favorite baseball team's managerial changeover, in a final comment before going to the California gas chamber:

"I'm very unhappy about the Giants. I didn't think Bill Rigney knew very much, but I don't think Tom Sheehan knows anything at all."

RICHIE ASHBURN
center fielder on the pennant-winning Philadelphia Phillies of 1950, on why the club had never won another pennant:

"We were all white."

ALBERT G. SPALDING
sportsman/businessman:

"Two hours is about as long as an American can wait for the close of a baseball game—or anything else, for that matter."

BILL VEECK
major league baseball owner, asked what would be his first act if he were named major league baseball commissioner:

"Resign."

HERBERT HOOVER
thirty-first President of the United States:

"Next to religion, baseball has had a greater impact on the American people than any other institution."

ROGER KAHN
writer:

"The rhythms of the game are so similar to the patterns of American life. Periods of leisure, interrupted by bursts of frantic activity."

GERALD BEAUMONT
writer:

"Baseball is a peculiar profession, possibly the only one which capitalized a boyhood pleasure, unfits the athlete for any other career, keeps him young in mind and spirit, and then rejects him as too old before he has yet attained the prime of life."

JOE GARAGIOLA
major league catcher-turned-sportscaster:

"Baseball gives you every chance to be great. Then it puts every pressure on you to prove that you haven't got what it takes. It never takes away the chance, and it never eases up on the pressure."

FRANK FRISCH
major league manager:

"Baseball is like this. Have one good year and you can fool them for five more, because for five more years they expect you to have another good one."

PETER GENT
writer:

"Baseball players are the weirdest of all. I think it's all that organ music."

CASEY STENGEL
New York Yankees manager:

"I don't like them fellas who drive in two runs and let in three."

BABE RUTH
New York Yankees outfielder, in response to a policeman who stopped him while driving and said, "This is a one-way street":

"I'm only *drivin'* one way!"

BOB GIBSON
St. Louis Cardinals pitcher:

"A great catch is like watching girls go by. The last one you see is always the prettiest."

BRANCH RICKEY
major league executive:

"Baseball is a game of inches."

RED SMITH
sportswriter:

"Ninety feet between bases is the nearest to perfection that man has yet achieved."

KURT ANDERSON
writer:

"We should worship nationally the heft, the stitching, the hard integrity of these wholesome little spheres. The baseball is pal and talisman both, and that's sublime."

JOE MCCARTHY
New York Yankees catcher:

"Give a boy a bat and a ball and a place to play and you'll have a good citizen."

BILL LEE
major league pitcher:

"In baseball, you're supposed to sit on your ass, spit tobacco and nod at stupid things."

JIM MURRAY
sportswriter, on whether baseball is a business:

"If it isn't, General Motors is a sport."

WILLIAM WRIGLEY
Chicago Cubs owner:

"Baseball is too much a sport to be a business and too much a business to be a sport."
   (Also attributed to Philip Wrigley and Branch Rickey)

JOE MCCARTHY
New York Yankees catcher:

"You can't freeze the ball in this game. You have to play till the last man is out."

ALBERT G. SPALDING
sportsman/businessman:

"I claim baseball owes its prestige as our national game to the fact that no other form of sport is such an exponent of American courage, confidence, combativeness, dash, discipline, determination, energy, eagerness, pluck, persistency, performance, spirit, sagacity, success, vim, vigor and virility."

ABBIE HOFFMAN
former Yippie leader, on eccentric baseball player Jimmy Piersall, who spent some time in a mental institution:

"He showed them it was a game, so they locked him up."

BEANO COOK
CBS Sports publicist and ardent football fan, after Bowie Kuhn gave the 52 released Iran hostages lifetime major league baseball passes:

"Haven't they suffered enough?"

JOE PEPITONE
New York Yankees outfielder:

"In center field, you've got too much time to think about everything but baseball."

TOMMY HENRICH
New York Yankees outfielder:

"Catching a fly ball is a pleasure, but knowing what to do with it after you catch it is a business."

BOBBY BRAGAN
Texas Rangers administrator, after a game against Toronto that featured a promotional appearance by Clayton Moore, television's original Lone Ranger:

"It's not very often we get to see the Lone Ranger and Toronto the same night."

ELIO CHACON
New York Mets shortstop, asked how his new sports car had sustained extensive damage, including smashed headlights and taillights, twisted fenders, a door handle missing and a cracked windshield:

"Parking."

FRANK FRISCH
St. Louis Cardinals player-manager:

"There's no room for sentiment in baseball if you want to win."

JOHNNY CARSON
the *Tonight* show host, when Pete Rose had hit in 38 consecutive games in pursuit of Joe DiMaggio's record:

"Thirty-eight going for 56! Sounds like Dolly Parton going through puberty."

TY COBB
Hall of Fame outfielder, explaining in 1960 why he thought he would hit only .300 against modern-day pitching:

"You've got to remember—I'm 73."

HEYWOOD BROUN
writer:

"The tradition of professional baseball always has been agreeably free of chivalry. The rule is, 'Do anything you can get away with.'"

CASEY STENGEL
major league manager:

"Now, there's three things you can do in a baseball game. You can win, or you can lose, or it can rain."

KIN HUBBARD
humorist:

"Knowin' all about baseball is just about as profitable as bein' a good whittler."

JIM MURRAY
sportswriter:

"Catching a fly ball, or hitting a curved one, is not all that difficult. It may rank in difficulty somewhere below juggling Indian clubs and above playing an ocarina."

BOB LEMON
major league manager:

"Baseball was made for kids, and grown-ups only screw it up."

RED SMITH
sportswriter:

"The baseball mind is a jewel in the strict sense—that is to say, a stone of special value, rare beauty and extreme hardness. Cut, polished and fixed in the Tiffany setting of a club owner's skull, it resists change as a diamond resists erosion."

BILL TERRY
Hall of Fame first baseman:

"Baseball must be a great game to survive the fools who run it."

ARTHUR DALEY
writer:

"Baseball must be a great game to survive the people who run it."

GENE MAUCH
California Angels manager:

"Baseball and malaria keep coming back."

E. B. WHITE
writer, in the postscript of a letter to friend and journalist Frank Sullivan:

"It is also necessary at this season to establish firm emotional connections with a major league ball club, to share in the agonies of their defeats and the ecstasies of their triumphs. Without these simple marriages, none of us could survive."

ROY CAMPANELLA
Brooklyn Dodgers catcher:

"You gotta be a man to play baseball for a living, but you gotta have a lot of little boy in you, too."

JIM MURRAY
sportswriter:

"Baseball is a game played by nine athletes on the field and 20 fast-buck artists in the front office."

JIM LONBORG
former major league pitcher:

"Baseball is such a great life that anyone who complains about it, I think, is a little clouded. I could never find the time to complain."

MAYO SMITH
major league manager:

"Open up a ballplayer's head and you know what you'd find? A lot of little broads and a jazz band."

TOMMY LASORDA
Los Angeles Dodgers manager:

"No matter how good you are, you're going to lose one-third of your games. No matter how bad you are, you're going to win one-third of your games. It's the other third that makes the difference."

JIM MURRAY
sportswriter, defining Little League:

" . . . a juvenile activity that makes delinquents out of adults."

WHITEY HERZOG
St. Louis Cardinals manager:

"Baseball has been very good to me since I quit trying to play it."

DAVID LARNER
Lloyd's of London representative and underwriter for most of the $50 million strike insurance purchased by major league owners prior to the 1981 season:

"Baseball? Rather like rounders, isn't it? Never saw the game myself. But I suppose the underwriters never actually saw the *Titanic,* either."

EARL WEAVER
Baltimore Orioles manager, after optioning outfielder Drungo Hazewood, who was hitting .583 in spring training:

"I've never cut a guy hitting that high before. But he was making the rest of us look bad with that average."

CESAR GERONIMO
Cincinnati Reds outfielder, on being the 3,000th strikeout victim of both Nolan Ryan and Bob Gibson:

"I was just in the right place at the right time."

MIKE SADEK
San Francisco Giants reserve catcher, on teammate Mike Ivie's two pinch-hit grand-slam homers in 1978:

"Why doesn't anyone give me credit? I'm the guy he pinch-hit for both times."

JIM MURRAY
sportswriter:

"A king may be a king because his father was, but a ballplayer is a major leaguer only so long as his averages show he is."

WILLIE STARGELL
Pittsburgh Pirates outfielder:

"Nobody ever said, 'Work ball!' They say, 'Play ball!' To me, that means having fun."

BASE STEALERS AND STEALING

LOU BROCK
St. Louis Cardinals outfielder-turned-broadcaster:

"It's almost like choosing weapons. The runner chooses, the pitcher chooses, you step off three paces and come out firing."

KEN COLEMAN
baseball broadcaster, after witnessing a long home run:

"They usually show movies on a flight like that."
(Paul Splittorff, Kansas City Royals pitcher, after seeing teammate George Brett smash a 420-foot home run:
"Anything that goes that far in the air ought to have a stewardess on it.")

MAURY WILLS
former Los Angeles Dodgers shortstop, on why he didn't steal home more often:

"Frank Howard used to say that if I tried anything funny like stealing home when he was up, he'd take my head off with his bat."

ARTHUR "BUGS" BAER
writer, on plodding base runner Ping Bodie:

"He had larceny in his heart, but his feet were honest."

DOC MEDICH
Milwaukee Brewers pitcher, on prolific base stealer Rickey Henderson of the Oakland A's:

"He's like a little kid in a train station. You turn your back on him and he's gone."

CATCHERS AND CATCHING

JEFF TORBORG
major league catcher:

"There must be some reason we're the only ones facing the other way."

STEVE YEAGER
Los Angeles Dodgers catcher:

"Why am I a catcher? Look at this equipment. You know what they call this stuff? The tools of ignorance. Does that answer the question?"

BOB UECKER
major league catcher-turned-broadcaster:

"The way to catch a knuckleball is to wait until the ball stops rolling and then pick it up."

BILL DELANCEY
St. Louis Cardinals catcher, to manager Frank Frisch, who wanted to know what pitch an opponent had clouted for a game-winning homer:

"How do I know? I haven't caught that pitch yet."

HANK GREENWALD
sportscaster, to San Francisco talk show host and onetime catcher Ken Dito:

"How many games was it before they told you about the mask?"

HITTERS AND HITTING

JOE SCHULTZ
Seattle Pilots manager:

"Well, boys, it's a round ball and a round bat and you got to hit it square."
    (Also attributed to Pete Rose)

TY COBB
Hall of Fame outfielder:

"Every great batter works on the theory that the pitcher is more afraid of him than he is of the pitcher."

PING BODIE
major league outfielder, after being struck out by the legendary Walter Johnson:

"You can't hit what you can't see."
   (Also attributed to Chicago Cubs infielder Joe Tinker in reference to the fastball of New York Giants pitcher Rube Marquard)

BUCKY HARRIS
Washington Senators manager, advising his weak-hitting team before it faced hard-throwing Cleveland Indians pitcher Bob Feller:

"Go up and hit what you see. And if you don't see it, come on back."

BOB UECKER
former major league catcher who registered a .200 lifetime batting average, on the pinnacle of his career:

"In 1967 with St. Louis, I walked with the bases loaded to drive in the winning run in an intrasquad game in spring training."

LEFTY GOMEZ
Hall of Fame pitcher but an inept hitter, recalling the only time in his career he broke a bat:

"I ran over it backing out of the garage."

HENRY AARON
former major league outfielder and recordholder for most career home runs:

"Babe Ruth always will be Number One. Before I broke his (home run) record it was the greatest of all. Then I broke it and suddenly the greatest record is Joe DiMaggio's hitting streak."

REGGIE JACKSON
major league outfielder, on facing Nolan Ryan:

"Every hitter likes fastballs, just like everybody likes ice cream. But you don't like it when someone's stuffing it into you by the gallon."

PEPPER MARTIN
St. Louis Cardinals infielder/outfielder, on why he removed the innersoles from his spikes:

"They make me too high and I'm hitting over the ball."

MICKEY MANTLE
Hall of Fame outfielder:

"During my 18 years I came to bat almost 10,000 times. I struck out about 1,700 times and walked maybe 1,800 times. You figure a ballplayer will average about 500 at bats a season. That means I played seven years in the major leagues without even hitting the ball."

(Norm Cash, former Detroit Tigers first baseman who set a team record with 1,081 career strikeouts: "Prorated at 500 at bats a year, that means that for two years out of the 14 I played, I never even touched the ball."

Reggie Jackson, major league outfielder: "When you play the game 10 years, go to bat 7,000 times and get 2,000 hits, you know what that means? It means that you've gone 0 for 5,000.")

WILLIE STARGELL
Pittsburgh Pirates outfielder:

"If I'm hitting, I can hit anyone. If not, my twelve-year-old son can get me out."

PEE WEE REESE
Brooklyn/Los Angeles Dodgers shortstop-turned-sportscaster:

"If I had my career to play over, one thing I'd do differently is swing more. Those 1,200 walks I got, nobody remembers them."

BABE RUTH
New York Yankees outfielder:

"All I can tell 'em is I pick a good one and sock it. I get back to the dugout and they ask me what it was I hit and I tell 'em I don't know except it looked good."

HENRY AARON
Milwaukee Braves outfielder, when he stepped up to bat during a 1957 World Series game only to have New York Yankees catcher Yogi Berra inform him his bat label wasn't facing up:

"I get paid for hitting, not for reading."

BILL BYRON
the "Singing Umpire," taunting a player after a called third strike:

Let me tell you something, son,
Before you get much older,
You cannot hit the ball, my friend,
With the bat upon your shoulder.

RALPH KINER
Hall of Fame outfielder, asked why he didn't choke up when he hit:

"Cadillacs are down at the end of the bat."

REGGIE JACKSON
major league outfielder:

"I'd rather hit than have sex."

BOBBY MURCER
major league outfielder, on batting slumps:

"You decide you'll wait for your pitch. Then, as the ball starts toward the plate you think about your stance; and then you think about your swing; and then you realize the ball that went past you for a strike was your pitch."

CHARLEY LAU
major league hitting instructor:

"There are two theories on hitting the knuckleball. Unfortunately, neither of them works."

ROBIN ROBERTS
Hall of Fame pitcher, describing his greatest All-Star game thrill:

"When Mickey Mantle bunted with the wind blowing out in Crosley Field."

DIZZY DEAN
major league pitcher, to a New York writer as they pulled into a gas station:

"It puzzles me how they know what corners are good for filling stations. Just how did these fellows know there was gas and oil under here?"

JIM BROSNAN
Cincinnati Reds relief pitcher, asked if it bothered him that most bullpens afford a poor view of the game:

"That's the best part of it."

PITCHERS AND PITCHING

EARLY WYNN
Hall of Fame pitcher:

"The space between the white lines—that's my office. That's where I conduct my business."

SANDY KOUFAX
Los Angeles Dodgers pitcher:

"Pitching is the art of instilling fear by making a man flinch."

BILLY LOES
Brooklyn Dodgers pitcher:

"Never win 20 games, because then they'll expect you to do it every year."

WARREN SPAHN
Milwaukee Braves pitcher:

"Hitting is timing. Pitching is upsetting timing."

JERRY HINSLEY
rookie New York Mets pitcher, after knocking down Willie Mays with his first pitch on the advice of teammates, but then yielding a booming triple to the Giants slugger:

"They didn't tell me what to throw him on the *second* pitch."

FERNANDO VALENZUELA
Los Angeles Dodgers pitcher, on why he looks skyward during his delivery:

"I don't want to see the hits going past me."

EARL WEAVER
Baltimore Orioles manager, on pitcher Mike Cuellar's complaint late in his career that he wasn't getting a chance to prove he still had it:

"I gave Mike more chances than I gave my first wife."

STEVE HOVLEY
Seattle Pilots outfielder:

"To a pitcher, a base hit is the perfect example of negative feedback."

DOYLE ALEXANDER
Baltimore Orioles relief pitcher, after pitching for the first time in a couple of weeks:

"When I got to the mound, catcher Johnny Oates reminded me that the lower mask was his and the upper one was the umpire's."

TIM McCARVER
St. Louis Cardinals catcher:

"Bob Gibson is the luckiest pitcher I ever saw. He always pitches when the other team doesn't score any runs."

JIM BOUTON
major league pitcher-turned-sportscaster/writer:

"You spend a good piece of your life gripping a baseball, and in the end it turns out that it was the other way around all the time."

CASEY STENGEL
major league manager:

"When a fielder gets a pitcher into trouble, the pitcher has to pitch himself out of a slump he isn't in."

EARLY WYNN
Hall of Fame pitcher, defending his reputation as "a guy who wouldn't give his own mother a good pitch to hit":

"Mother was a hell of a hitter."

CLAUDE "SKIP" LOCKWOOD
Seattle Pilots pitcher, asking teammate Jim Bouton for advice:

"Say, Jim, how do you hold your doubles?"

BILL KLEM
major league umpire, in response to rookie pitcher Johnny Sain, who protested after three close pitches to slugger Rogers Hornsby were called balls:

"Young man, when you pitch a strike, Mr. Hornsby will let you know."

RALPH KINER
Hall of Fame outfielder, on how dull it is watching knuckleball pitchers:

"It's like watching Mario Andretti park a car."

BIRDIE TEBBETTS
Cleveland Indians manager, comparing rookie pitchers to veterans:

"It's the difference between a carpenter and a cabinetmaker."

LEFTY GOMEZ
Hall of Fame pitcher, asked if he ever threw a spitter:

"Not intentionally, but I sweat easy."

JOE HORLEN
Chicago White Sox pitcher, asked what he threw to Boston's Tony Conigliaro, who had homered to beat him 1–0:

"It was a baseball."

DON NEWCOMBE
Brooklyn Dodgers pitcher, asked what pitch Tommy Henrich had hit for a homer to give the Yankees a 1–0 victory in game one of the 1952 World Series:

"A change of space."

CASEY STENGEL
major league manager:

"If it breaks over the plate, it ain't a curve ball."

WARREN SPAHN
Hall of Fame pitcher, recalling the pitch he threw to rookie Willie Mays that resulted in the young outfielder's first major league hit, a blast over the left-field roof at the Polo Grounds:

"For the first 60 feet it was a hell of a pitch."

(Spahn, noting that Mays was "something like 0 for 21" at the time: "I'll never forgive myself. We might have gotten rid of Willie forever if I'd only struck him out.")

SATCHEL PAIGE
Hall of Fame pitcher, on why he called one of his most reliable pitches his "be ball":

"Because it always be where I want it to be."

SPARKY LYLE
major league relief pitcher, on why he prefers not being a starter:

"Why pitch nine innings when you can get just as famous pitching two?"

TUG MCGRAW
Philadelphia Phillies relief pitcher, on the vicissitudes of his craft:

"Some days you tame the tiger. And some days the tiger has you for lunch."

JIM BOUTON
former major league pitcher; during preparation for a comeback at age 38:

"This winter I'm working out every day, throwing at a wall. I'm 11 and 0 against the wall."

CASEY STENGEL
New York Mets manager, to Mets pitcher Ray Daviault, who was complaining that an opponent had hit "a perfect pitch" for a home run:

"It couldn't have been a perfect pitch. Perfect pitches don't travel that far."

DON SUTTON
Los Angeles Dodgers pitcher, recalling an encounter with pitcher Gaylord Perry:

"He handed me a tube of Vaseline. I thanked him and gave him a sheet of sandpaper."

CASEY STENGEL
New York Yankees manager, asked after Don Larsen's perfect game against the Brooklyn Dodgers in the 1956 World Series if it was the best game he had ever seen Larsen pitch:

"So far."

DON LARSEN
former New York Yankees pitcher, asked if he ever gets tired of talking about his 1956 World Series perfect game:

"No, why should I?"

CY YOUNG
Hall of Fame pitcher, to a reporter:

"I won more games than you ever saw."

TOMMY LASORDA
Los Angeles Dodgers manager:

"There are three types of baseball players—those who make it happen, those who watch it happen, and those who wonder what happens."

Basketball

ART RUST
sportscaster:

"If cocaine were helium, the whole NBA would float away."

TOM HEINSOHN
former Boston Celtics coach, on the NBA playoffs:

"They go on and on and on. It's like a guy telling a bad joke for 15 minutes."

MIKE NEWLIN
New Jersey Nets sharpshooting guard, asked why he was wearing gloves:

"You put your money in a wallet, don't you?"

RED AUERBACH
Boston Celtics general manager:

"Basketball is like war in that offensive weapons are developed first, and it always takes awhile for the defense to catch up."

GARY WILLIAMS
American University basketball coach:

"Playgrounds are the best place to learn the game, because if you lose, you sit down."

LEE ROSE
University of North Carolina at Charlotte basketball coach:

"I would like to deny the statement that I think basketball is a matter of life and death. I feel it's much more important than that."

STEVE KELLEY
sportswriter:

"In the NBA, nothing recedes like success."

DWANE MORRISON
Georgia Tech basketball coach:

"Everywhere I go there's interest in Georgia Tech basketball. But then, I only go to places where there's interest in Georgia Tech basketball."

WELDON DREW
New Mexico State basketball coach, explaining his team's slow start:

"We have a great bunch of outside shooters. Unfortunately, all of our games are played indoors."

TOM HEINSOHN
former Boston Celtics forward, on why he turned down a football scholarship:

"If I was going to get beat up, I wanted it to be indoors where it was warm."

PETE NEWELL
Golden State Warriors scout:

"When I was young, college basketball was an extension of the college itself. Now it is a piece of some television network."

RED AUERBACH
Boston Celtics general manager, on why basketball is a simple game:

"The ball is round and the floor is smooth."

LYLE DAMON
San Francisco State basketball coach, informed that opponents were shooting a mere .579 from the free-throw line:

"We defend against the free throw very well."

JOHNNY KERR
sportscaster and former NBA player and coach, on how he would guard Kareem Abdul-Jabbar:

"I'd get real close to him and breathe on his goggles."

HOT ROD HUNDLEY
Los Angeles Laker-turned-sportscaster:

"My biggest thrill came the night Elgin Baylor and I combined for 73 points in Madison Square Garden. Elgin had 71 of them."

●

BILL RUSSELL
former Boston Celtics center, who in two decades went from being the only black on the Celtics to serving as coach and general manager of the predominantly black Seattle SuperSonics:

"In basketball, it took only 20 years to go from the outhouse to the in crowd."

Boasts

MUHAMMAD ALI
three-time heavyweight boxing champion:

"When you're as great as I am, it's hard to be humble."

AL OLIVER
major league first baseman:

"There's no such thing as bragging. You're either lying or telling the truth."

DEREK SANDERSON
Boston Bruins center, asked to name the greatest hockey player he ever saw:

"Me—on instant replay."

WENDELL TYLER
Los Angeles Rams running back, asked what NFL runner he most admires:

"Myself, because I've come such a long way."

DIZZY DEAN
Hall of Fame pitcher:

"I may not have been the greatest pitcher ever, but I was amongst 'em."

TRENT TUCKER
Minnesota basketball guard, on his shooting range:

"All I have to be is in the arena."

DARRYL DAWKINS
Philadelphia 76ers center famous for breaking backboards with his slam dunks:

"It takes one hell of a man to bring all that glass down, and that's just what I proclaim to be."

MUHAMMAD ALI
three-time heavyweight boxing champion, claiming he would win the title a fourth time:

"I'll be greater than all the stars in Hollywood. They'll make cartoons about me. I'll be inhuman!"

BOBBY FISCHER
world chess champion:

"There's only one immortal player in the world today and it is Fischer. It's nice to be modest, but it's stupid not to tell the truth."

LARRY BIRD
Boston Celtics forward, addressing teammates at a celebration of the Celtics' 1981 NBA championship:

"I could stand up here all night talking about the whole team. But I'm getting sick and tired of talking about myself."

BO BELINSKY
Los Angeles Angels pitcher, after throwing a no-hitter:

"My only regret in life is that I can't sit in the stands and watch me pitch."

REGGIE JACKSON
major league outfielder:

"The only reason I don't like playing in the World Series is I can't watch myself play."

TOMMY LASORDA
Los Angeles Dodgers manager, after Dodgers pitcher Jerry Reuss tossed a no-hitter:

"It couldn't have happened to a greater guy. Well—yes, it could. It could have happened to me."

BILL RUSSELL
former Boston Celtics center, asked how he would have fared against Kareem Abdul-Jabbar:

"Young man, you have the question backwards."

TED TURNER
Atlanta Braves and Hawks owner:

"If I only had a little humility I would be perfect."

Boxers and Boxing

KEN NORTON
professional boxer:

"Boxing is a great sport and a dirty business."

AL BRAVERMAN
fight manager, accused of having his
boxers use a foreign substance on
their gloves:

"It's not a foreign substance.
It's made right here in the
United States."

SUGAR RAY ROBINSON
former welterweight and middleweight champion:

"Hurting people is my business."

DREW "BUNDINI" BROWN
trainer, describing Muhammad Ali's fighting style in an imperative that became
one of Ali's credos:

"Float like a butterfly, sting like a bee."

DOC KEARNS
fight manager, on boxer Mickey
Walker's hobby of painting:

"It's the only thing that could
keep Mickey Walker on
canvas."

ROCKY GRAZIANO
former middleweight champion:

"Fighting is the only racket where you're almost guaranteed to
end up as a bum."

JERRY PERENCHIO
sports promoter:

"If there's a wrinkle here and a straight deal there, the boxing
crowd would go for the wrinkle every time."

BOB BIRON
fight manager:

"When it's all finished and I write a book, if I do, the title will
be *The Only Thing Square Was the Ring*."

GEORGE FOREMAN
heavyweight champion:

"Boxing is sort of like jazz. The better it is, the less amount of
people can appreciate it."

THEODORE ROOSEVELT
twenty-sixth President of the United States:

"I do but little boxing because it seems rather absurd for a President to appear with a black eye or a swollen nose or a cut lip."

ED "TOO TALL" JONES
Dallas Cowboys defensive lineman, on his brief career in boxing:

"I have never been around so many crummy people in all my days."

KONRAD LORENZ
Austrian ethologist:

"Few lapses of self-control are punished as immediately and severely as loss of temper during a boxing bout."

WILLIE PEP
former featherweight champion, on the stages of a boxer's decline:

"First your legs go. Then you lose your reflexes. Then you lose your friends."

LENNY MANCINI
professional boxer, characterizing his vocation:

"One day headlines, the next day breadlines."

FLOYD PATTERSON
former heavyweight champion, late in his career:

"If one guy has one fight left in him, he seems to save it for me."

MAX BAER
former heavyweight champion:

"If you ever get belted and see three fighters through a haze, go after the one in the middle. That's what ruined me—I went after the two guys on the end."

JIM MURRAY
sportswriter:

"Well, I see where boxing's long-playing record, that master of the diplomatic quote, that tower of modesty, Cassius Clay, has announced he could knock out Jack Dempsey in two rounds. That figures. Dempsey is 69 years old. Jack Johnson probably wouldn't last that long. Johnson is dead."

DANIEL GONZALES
Argentine boxer, asked if Sugar Ray Leonard, who had knocked him out in the first round, was the best man he had ever fought:

"I don't know. I wasn't in there long enough to find out."

BRUCE WOODCOCK
boxer, revealing which punch bothered him most after being knocked out by Tami Mauriello:

"The last one."

WILLIE PASTRANO
light heavyweight boxer, in response to a ring doctor who asked if he knew where he was after José Torres knocked him down in a 1965 title bout:

"You're damn right I know where I am. I'm in Madison Square Garden getting beaten up."

MUHAMMAD ALI
three-time heavyweight boxing champion, prior to his 1980 bout with reigning WBC champion Larry Holmes:

"Musically speaking, if Holmes don't C-sharp, he'll B-flat."

ANONYMOUS NEW YORK FIGHT FAN
after Muhammad Ali's 1971 loss at Madison Square Garden to Joe Frazier:

"Why should I feel sorry for Ali? He got $2.5 million for being beaten up. Most of us in this city have to pay for that privilege."

ALVA JOHNSTON
writer, on heavyweight champion James J. Corbett:

"His pupils reported that to box with him was to participate in a fight between the past and the future: their punches always landed at points that he had vacated long before."

JIM MURRAY
sportswriter:

"The early rounds of an [Archie] Moore fight always remind me of a guy opening the hood of an engine and exploring around inside for weak spots. Only, when he finds them, he doesn't repair them. He makes them worse. It's a trick a lot of mechanics have, but with Dr. Moore it's a high art. A loose bolt here, a sticky valve there, and by the time Arch has gotten through tinkering, the transmission falls out."

ARCHIE MOORE
light-heavyweight champion, in response to middleweight champion Paul Pender's demand for a shot at Moore's title:

"For me to meet a man like that and face my conscience, I would have to agree to let him carry a pistol."

BUSTER MATHIS
heavyweight boxer, asked what his handlers do:

"All I know is when the bell rings I walk up the steps and they walk down the steps."

JAKE LAMOTTA
former middleweight champion, reflecting on his five bouts with Sugar Ray Robinson:

"I fought Sugar Ray so many times it's a wonder I didn't get diabetes."

TULLUS MEAD
Tennessee high school coach, comparing his 1952 Golden Gloves fight with Sonny Liston to the 1962 Liston–Floyd Patterson fight:

"When Liston hit Patterson he stayed down and collected a fortune. When Liston hit me, like a fool I got up and he hit me again."

A. J. LIEBLING
writer, recalling how Joe Louis used to heed his advice:

" 'Let him have it, Joe,' I would yell whenever I saw him fight, and sooner or later he would let the other fellow have it."

Broadcasters

JOHN SCHULIAN
sportswriter:

"I think America's television sportscasters are given a choice when they embark upon their careers. They can either have brains or blow-dryers."

RALPH EDWARDS
broadcaster:

"Marconi invented radio, but Ted Husing knew what to do with it."

JIMMY CANNON
sportswriter, on sportscaster Harry Wismer:

"He announces a football game like a holdup victim hollering for a cop."

BILL CURRIE
sportscaster, on the role of broadcasting's color man:

"He's a guy paid to talk while everyone else goes to the bathroom."

JIM MURRAY
sportswriter, on sportscaster Graham McNamee:

"He didn't know much about sports. But he was a demon on meteorology. He could do 40 minutes on the changing of a leaf color. It was said he went through an entire Rose Bowl game without once alluding to the action on the field. The snow-capped mountains, the Rose Queen, the floats and the movie stars were enough for Graham."

RING LARDNER
writer, after sitting next to sports caster Graham McNamee at a 1924 World Series game, the first-ever radio broadcast direct from the site of play:

"The Washington Senators and the New York Giants must have played a doubleheader this afternoon—the game I saw and the game Graham McNamee announced."

CHRIS SHENKEL
sportscaster, to viewers of a high school game while officials and players were trotting down the field to change sides after the first quarter:

"The penalty is on Montclair."

DON DUNPHY
fight announcer, identifying a boxer during a telecast:

"Hallacy is the boxer in the green trunks and the red blood."

JIM MURRAY
sportswriter, on Howard Cosell:

"He's pedantic, he sounds condescending, but he actually flatters his audience by using words that seem more suitable to the *Yale Law Review* than the Green Bay Packers. He never rushes his words. He pontificates, and his words come down as if meant to be graven on stone, or linked with the Sermon on the Mount. He was a lawyer by trade and is miscast for any show that doesn't give him plenty of landing room for his flights of fancy."

JIMMY CANNON
sportswriter, on Howard Cosell:

"He changed his name from Cohen to Cosell, put on a toupee and 'tells it like it is.'"

HARRY CARAY
sportscaster:

"I tell it like it is. Howard Cosell tells it like Roone Arledge wants it told."

ANONYMOUS SPORTSWRITER
on the boundless optimism of St. Louis Blues announcer Dan Kelly:

"If he were on the *Titanic*, he'd spend half of his time telling about what great swimmers were on board."

BILL STERN
sportscaster, making history at a 1939 baseball game between Columbia University and Princeton:

"Good afternoon, ladies and gentlemen. Welcome to the first telecast of a sporting event. I'm not sure what it is we're doing here, but I certainly hope it turns out well for you people who are watching." (Station W2XBS, New York)

JIMMY POWERS
TV fight announcer, offering viewers an explanation for why Sugar Ray Robinson might have inadvertently punched Paul Pender after the 13th-round bell in their 1960 middleweight championship bout:

"It's hard to hear the bell up there. There's a tremendous amount of smoke here in Boston Garden."

JIMMY DEMARET
television commentator at the 1964 Crosby, explaining the predicament of Arnold Palmer, who had hit his tee shot on the 17th into the ocean:

"His nearest drop from there would be Honolulu."

Character

GERALD R. FORD
thirty-eighth President of the United States:

"If it is a cliché to say athletics build character as well as muscle, then I subscribe to the cliché."

HEYWOOD HALE BROUN
writer/broadcaster:

"Sports do not build character. They reveal it."

PEPPER RODGERS
college football coach-turned-sportscaster:

"Coaches like to talk about building character. They don't build character. They eliminate those who don't have it."

JOHN WOODEN
UCLA basketball coach:

"Ability may get you to the top, but it takes character to keep you there."

WALTER CAMP
Yale football coach:

"There is no substitute for hard work and effort beyond the call of mere duty. That is what strengthens the soul and ennobles one's character."

LARRY KING
writer:

"Pro football is a mean game, ideally played by mean men. If it builds character, so does street mugging."

PHIL MALONEY
Vancouver Canucks coach and general manager:

"I try for good players and I try for good character. If necessary, though, I settle for the player."

TOM LANDRY
Dallas Cowboys coach:

"A team that has character doesn't need stimulation."

JOHN WOODEN
UCLA basketball coach:

"Be more concerned with your character than with your reputation, because your character is what you really are, while your reputation is merely what others think you are."

RAY MALAVASI
Los Angeles Rams coach:

"They say losing builds character. I have all the character I need."

Cheating

DARRYL ROGERS
Arizona State football coach:

"They'll fire you for losing before they'll fire you for cheating."

CHI CHI RODRIGUEZ
professional golfer:

"For most amateurs, the best wood in the bag is the pencil."

JIM MURRAY
sportswriter:

"When you get in the hole, and mark your score, you say, 'I had a 5 there.' Then you look around, and if no one is looking at you funny you frown and start to erase saying, 'No, that's not right, it was only a 4.' This is known in golf as improving your lie. In other words, the first score was a lie, but the second was a better one."

ROBERT MAYNARD HUTCHINS
University of Chicago president, in 1939, on why he was abolishing the school's football program:

"To be successful, one must cheat. Everyone is cheating and I refuse to cheat."

Childhood Days

BILL RUSSELL
former Boston Celtics center:

"When I was growing up, my mother wouldn't allow me to go near a golf course. She didn't think the people who played were very nice. Now I play every day, and you know what? She was right."

LOU BROCK
St. Louis Cardinals outfielder:

"When I was a kid, I used to imagine animals running under my bed. I told my dad and he solved the problem quickly. He cut the legs off the bed."

JOE JARES
sportswriter:

"Not that it helped me much in childhood frays, but I was the only kid on my block who could boast, with absolutely no fear of contradiction, 'My father can lick your father.' Frank August Jares, Sr., was a professional wrestler, the nastiest, meanest, basest, most arrogant, cheatingest, bloodthirstiest eye-gouger around. No rule, referee or sense of fair play ever hampered his style. In short, the sort of man a boy could look up to."

DANNY MURTAUGH
major league infielder, to a heckling fan:

"When I was a youngster, I lived on a farm. We had a jackass on that farm that just wouldn't do anything. One day I really gave that jackass a beating. My father heard the jackass hollering and came to his rescue. Then he turned on me and gave me a good lacing for what I had done. His last words were, 'Someday that jackass is going to haunt you.' And, you know, up till now I never did believe him."

RODNEY DANGERFIELD
comedian, on how tough his childhood neighborhood was:

"You'd see guys bowling overhand."

LEE TREVINO
professional golfer:

"My family was so poor they couldn't afford any kids. The lady next door had me."

DAVID "SMOKEY" GAINES
San Diego State basketball coach:

"We were so poor, every time my mother tossed the dog a bone, he had to signal for a fair catch, else all us kids would beat him to it."

BUM PHILLIPS
professional football coach:

"When I was a kid, our land was so poor we had to fertilize the house just to raise the windows."

JAKE LAMOTTA
professional boxer:

"We were so poor, every Christmas eve my old man would go outside and shoot his gun, then come in and tell us kids that Santa Claus had committed suicide."

Cities and Towns

REGGIE JACKSON
California Angels outfielder:

"The only trouble with Baltimore is it's in Baltimore."

JIM MURRAY
sportswriter:

"The only trouble with Spokane, Washington, as a city is that there's nothing to do there after 10 o'clock. In the morning."

RICHIE SCHEINBLUM
Cleveland Indians outfielder:

"The only good thing about playing in Cleveland is you don't have to make road trips there."

LOU HOLTZ
Arkansas football coach, on the school's locale:

"Fayetteville isn't the end of the world, but you can see it from there."

GEORGE SCOTT
major league first baseman:

"I didn't like playing in Milwaukee. I didn't go out there for a year. I hated to walk the streets or eat the food there. The people don't look right, like they were from London, Jamaica or another planet. I don't like the town. The only place worse is Cleveland."

AL MCGUIRE
former Marquette basketball coach:

"I come from New York, where if you fall down, someone will pick you up by your wallet."

MIKE FLANAGAN
Baltimore Orioles pitcher:

"I could never play in New York. The first time I ever came into a game there, I got in the bullpen car and they told me to lock the doors."

JIM MURRAY
sportswriter, on Cincinnati:

"It looks like it's in the midst of condemnation proceedings. If it was human, they'd bury it.

"You have to think that when Dan'l Boone was fighting the Indians for this territory, he didn't have Cincinnati in mind for it. I wouldn't arm-wrestle Frank Finch for it. To give you an idea, the guys were kidding on the bus coming in to Cincinnati one time; and they decided that if war came, the Russians would bypass the city because they'd think it had already been bombed and taken."

MIKE SCHMIDT
Philadelphia Phillies third baseman:

"Philadelphia is the only city in the world where you can experience the thrill of victory and the agony of reading about it the next day."

DON KLOSTERMAN
Kansas City Chiefs scout, on life in Kansas City:

"It's a little like living in purgatory. It's not exactly heaven, but it isn't hell."

TERRY BRADSHAW
Pittsburgh Steelers quarterback, on Pittsburgh:

"I'd want this town on my side if we had to go to war again."

BOB PRINCE
sportscaster, on the undesirability of San Diego from a baseball announcer's perspective:

"In San Diego you have the Pacific Ocean to the west, Mexico to the south, the desert to the east, and Vin Scully to the north."

JIM MURRAY
sportswriter, on the self-proclaimed golf capital of the world:

"Palm Springs is an inland sandbar man has wrested from the rodents and the Indians to provide a day camp for over-privileged adults."

MIKE KRUKOW
major league pitcher who went from the Chicago Cubs to the Philadelphia Phillies to the San Francisco Giants in three years:

"People ask me where I live and I tell them, 'In escrow.' "

JOHNNY MAJORS
Tennessee football coach, on why the Tennessee hamlets of Lynchburg and Huntland are called "poke and plum" towns:

"If you poke your head out the car window, you are plum through town before you get it back inside."

LAVELL EDWARDS
Brigham Young football coach, after losing to host Wyoming in a snowstorm:

"I'd rather lose and live in Provo than win and live in Laramie."

GEORGE REVELING
Washington State basketball coach, on the remoteness of Pullman, Washington:

"My last speech was reviewed in *Field and Stream*."

MONTE CLARK
Detroit Lions coach, on his hometown, Kingsburg, California:

"It's a very small town. So small, in fact, that the number one industry there is taking bottles back to the store."

STAN HACK
former Chicago Cubs manager, on his hometown, Grand de Tour, Illinois:

"It's so small we don't even have a town drunk. Everyone has to take a turn."

JOHN CAMPBELL
Clemson basketball center, on his hometown, Blenheim, South Carolina:

"I think the population is only eight. No, make that six. One guy died last week and I'm out of town."

BOB UECKER
major league catcher-turned-sportscaster on life in Sun City, Arizona:

"At the ball games, the fans stand up for the National Anthem, and by the sixth inning they're just sitting back down."

Classics

BOB FITZSIMMONS
heavyweight boxer:

"The bigger they are, the harder they fall."

Sometimes quoted, "The bigger they come, the harder they fall." Fitzsimmons, who had surrendered his heavyweight crown to Jim Jeffries in an 1899 bout, made this taunting remark prior to a rematch in San Francisco on July 25, 1902. But Jeffries didn't fall. Outweighing Fitzsimmons by 39 pounds, the champion knocked out the challenger in the eighth round.

RED SANDERS
Vanderbilt football coach:

"Winning isn't everything, it's the only thing."

One of the best-known quotations ever to emerge from the sporting world. But the line belongs to Sanders, not, as is widely believed, to former NFL coach Vince Lombardi. Sanders' era was earlier than Lombardi's. Moreover, Lombardi himself repeatedly denied ever having made the statement. In his 1973 book *Vince Lombardi on Football*, Vol. 1, Lombardi asserts, "What I said is that 'Winning is not everything—but making the effort to win is.'"

LEO DUROCHER
Brooklyn Dodgers manager:

"Nice guys finish last."

Quoted by sportswriter Frank Graham in a 1948 article in the New York *Journal-American.* By Durocher's own account, he was in the Dodger dugout at the Polo Grounds chatting with several baseball writers prior to a game with the last-place New York Giants. Graham asked him why he was so high on Eddie Stanky, a fiercely competitive player of marginal ability. Durocher, in a lengthy response, said he liked Stanky's temperament. To punctuate his explanation, he nodded in the direction of the Giants as they emerged from their dugout to take their warm-ups. "Take a look at them," the Dodger manager said. "All nice guys. They'll finish last. Nice guys. Finish last."

Graham, a meticulous journalist, reported the remark accurately in his newspaper account the next day. But, according to Durocher, other writers who had been present "ran two sentences together to make it sound as if I were saying that you couldn't be a decent person and succeed."

JACK NORWORTH
lyricist:

"Take me out to the ball game."
The first line of the song that has become baseball's unofficial anthem. "Take Me Out to the Ball Game" was introduced in vaudeville in 1908. Albert von Tilzer composed the music some 20 years before he saw his first baseball game. The song was sung by Ann Sheridan and Dennis Morgan in the 1944 motion picture *Shine On Harvest Moon,* and a 1949 movie starring Gene Kelly, Esther Williams and Frank Sinatra took the song's title for its name.
The complete lyrics:

Take Me Out to the Ball Game

Take me out to the ball game,
Take me out to the park—
Buy me some peanuts and cracker jack,
I don't care if I never come back.
Let me root, root, root for the home team,
If they don't win it's a shame.
For it's one, two, three strikes, "You're out!"
At the old ball game.

GRANTLAND RICE
sportswriter:

For when the One Great Scorer comes to mark against your name,
He writes—not that you won or lost—but how you played the Game.

The final lines of Rice's poem "Alumnus Football." This verse spawned the popular credo, "It's not whether you win or lose, but how you play the game."

WEE WILLIE KEELER
Brooklyn Dodgers diminutive (5'4½") outfielder, on the art of hitting:

"Keep your eye on the ball and hit 'em where they ain't."
Keeler rode this technique into baseball's Hall of Fame with a .345 lifetime batting average. The line is sometimes quoted, "Keep your eye clear and hit 'em where they ain't." Most current references are abbreviated to, simply, "Hit 'em where they ain't."

TONY GALENTO
heavyweight boxer, before his 1939 title bout in New York with champion
Joe Louis:

"I'll moider de bum."

He didn't. Louis knocked him out in the fourth round, but the remark
has inexplicably enjoyed lasting renown and is entered in the fifteenth
edition of *Bartlett's Familiar Quotations*.

CHARLIE DRESSEN
Brooklyn Dodgers manager:

"The Giants is dead."

This pronouncement has lived in infamy since its utterance in 1951
when Dressen's Dodgers were in first place and the Giants were 13½
games back. The remark would have been quickly forgotten but for its
inaccuracy. The Giants staged a magnificent stretch drive to tie the Dodgers for first in the regular season, and then beat Brooklyn for the National
League pennant on Bobby Thomson's dramatic ninth-inning home run in
the third game of the play-offs.

HARRY STEVENS
ball park concessionaire:

"You can't tell the players without a scorecard."

BILL TERRY
New York Giants manager:

"Is Brooklyn still in the league?"

A facetious, rhetorical question posed by the gloating Giants manager
at a press conference in New York prior to the 1934 season. Terry was
responding to a journalist's inquiry as to how the Dodgers would fare
under new manager Casey Stengel. The previous year, the Dodgers had
finished sixth, 26½ games behind the world champion Giants.

As the 1934 season entered its final days, Terry and his Giants found
themselves tied for the National League lead with the St. Louis Cardinals.
The Giants final two games were against the Dodgers, who were again
floundering in sixth place. Remembering Terry's smug remark, Brooklyn
beat the Giants twice, 5–1 and 8–5, preventing their rivals from winning
a second straight pennant. Dodger fans in attendance at the Polo
Grounds flaunted banners that read, "Yes, We're Still in the League."

ERNEST LAWRENCE THAYER
writer/poet:

"But there is no joy in Mudville—mighty Casey has Struck Out."

The final line of Thayer's poem "Casey at the Bat," which first appeared in the San Francisco *Examiner* of June 3, 1888. The poem bore

the author's own subtitle, "A Ballad of the Republic." The original poem in its entirety:

Casey at the Bat

The outlook wasn't brilliant for the Mudville nine that day;
The score stood four to two with but one inning more to play;
And then, when Cooney died at first, and Barrows did the same,
A sickly silence fell upon the patrons of the game.

A struggling few got up to go, in deep despair. The rest
Clung to that hope which "springs eternal in the human breast";
They thought, If only Casey could but get a whack at that,
We'd put up even money now, with Casey at the bat.

But Flynn preceded Casey, as did also Jimmy Blake,
And the former was a lulu and the latter was a cake;
So, upon that stricken multitude grim melancholy sat,
For there seemed but little chance of Casey's getting to the bat.

But Flynn let drive a single, to the wonderment of all,
And Blake, the much despised, tore the cover off the ball,
And when the dust had lifted and men saw what had occurred,
There was Jimmy safe at second, and Flynn a-huggin' third.

Then from five thousand throats and more there rose a lusty yell,
It rumbled through the valley; it rattled in the dell;
It knocked upon the mountain and recoiled upon the flat,
For Casey, mighty Casey, was advancing to the bat.

There was ease in Casey's manner as he stepped into his place;
There was pride in Casey's bearing and a smile on Casey's face,
And when, responding to the cheers, he lightly doffed his hat,
No stranger in the crowd could doubt 'twas Casey at the bat.

Ten thousand eyes were on him as he rubbed his hands with dirt;
Five thousand tongues applauded when he wiped them on his shirt.
Then, while the writhing pitcher ground the ball into his hip,
Defiance gleamed in Casey's eye, a sneer curled Casey's lip.

And now the leather-covered sphere came hurtling through the air,
And Casey stood a-watching it in haughty grandeur there,
Close by the sturdy batsman the ball unheeded sped—
"That ain't my style," said Casey. "Strike one," the umpire said.

From the benches, black with people, there went up a muffled roar,
Like the beating of the storm-waves on a stern and distant shore.
"Kill him; kill the umpire!" shouted someone from the stand;
And it's likely they'd have killed him had not Casey raised his hand.

With a smile of Christian charity great Casey's visage shone;
He stilled the rising tumult; he bade the game go on;
He signaled to the pitcher, and once more the spheroid flew;
But Casey still ignored it, and the umpire said, "Strike two."

"Fraud," cried the maddened thousands, and echo answered "Fraud,"
But one scornful look from Casey, and the multitude was awed.
They saw his face grow stern and cold; they saw his muscles strain,
And they knew that Casey wouldn't let that ball go by again.

The sneer is gone from Casey's lip; his teeth are clenched in hate;
He pounds with cruel violence his bat upon the plate.
And now the pitcher holds the ball, and now he lets it go,
And now the air is shattered by the force of Casey's blow.

Oh! somewhere in this favored land the sun is shining bright;
The band is playing somewhere, and somewhere hearts are light.
And somewhere men are laughing, and somewhere children shout;
But there is no joy in Mudville—mighty Casey has Struck Out.

JOE JACOBS
fight manager:

"I shoulda stood in bed."

Another unremarkable utterance that not only has survived nearly half a century but has transcended sports, landed in *Bartlett's* and gained currency in our everyday language. Jacobs made the remark after leaving his sickbed to attend a 1935 World Series game and betting on the loser.

ANONYMOUS YOUNG BOY
to Shoeless Joe Jackson when the Chicago White Sox left fielder emerged from a courtroom after testifying in the grand jury investigation of the 1919 Black Sox scandal:

"Say it ain't so, Joe."

Both the accuracy and the authenticity of this quote remain widely disputed. The remark appeared in papers throughout the country, though some believe it was either the product of hearsay or an intentional fabrication by reporters. It was reported as "It isn't true, is it, Joe?" in the New York *Herald-Tribune;* "It ain't true, is it, Joe?" in the Chicago *Herald;* "Say it ain't so, Joe, say it ain't so" in the Chicago *Daily News;* "It ain't so, Joe, is it?" in the New York *Evening World;* and elsewhere, "You coulda made us proud, Joe."

Jackson consistently denied that any such remark was ever addressed to him. "There weren't any words passed between anybody except me and a deputy sheriff . . . ," he once said. "He asked me for a ride, and we got in the car together and left. There was a big crowd hanging around in front of the building, but nobody else said anything to me."

Ultimately, then, Shoeless Joe Jackson did indeed say it wasn't so.

FRANKLIN P. ADAMS
journalist/humorist:

These are the saddest of possible words, "Tinker to Evers to Chance."
Trio of bear cubs, and fleeter than birds, "Tinker to Evers to Chance."
Ruthlessly pricking our gonfalon bubble,

Making a Giant hit into a double—
Words that are heavy with nothing but trouble: "Tinker to Evers to Chance."

Joe Tinker, Johnny Evers and Frank Chance made up the Chicago Cubs' prolific double-play combination in the early 1900s. The three infielders were voted into baseball's Hall of Fame as a unit.

The poem, entitled "Baseball's Sad Lexicon," first appeared in the New York *Mail* in July, 1910.

JOHN L. SULLIVAN
heavyweight boxing champion:

"I can lick any man in the house."

Also quoted, "I can beat any son-of-a-bitch in the house." This boast was a favorite of Sullivan's, often uttered in crowded saloons. Sullivan won the last bareknuckle title, defeating Jake Kilrain in Richburg, Mississippi, in July, 1889.

JOE JACOBS
fight manager:

"We wuz robbed!"

Another unwitting passport to *Bartlett's Familiar Quotations* for Jacobs, who was outraged when his fighter, Max Schmeling, was stripped of his heavyweight championship by Jack Sharkey in a 15-round decision in New York in June, 1932.

KNUTE ROCKNE
Notre Dame football coach:

"Win one for the Gipper."

If this is, as has been suggested by *Sports Illustrated,* "One of the hoariest of sporting clichés," it is also one of the most debated. It is reasonably clear that Rockne did indeed, in so many words, exhort his team to win a 1928 game against Army in honor of George Gipp, which the Irish did in a stunning 12–6 upset. Gipp was a Notre Dame football star who fell ill and died quite suddenly following the 1920 season.

What is less clear is whether Gipp actually made a deathbed request of Rockne, imploring the coach to someday, "when the going isn't so easy, when the odds are against us, ask a Notre Dame team to win a game for me—for the Gipper. I don't know where I'll be then, Rock, but I'll know about it and I'll be happy."

It is widely believed that this poignant scene actually occurred; it is also widely believed that it didn't—that Rockne invented the scenario to motivate a downtrodden team.

Sportswriter Grantland Rice claimed Rockne personally told him the deathbed story in intimate detail on the eve of the now-famous Army game. Perhaps the coach was rehearsing. Sportswriter Paul Gallico wrote, "Actually, the real deathbed story was quite different. Rockne, holding the boy's hand, said, 'It must be tough to go, George.' To which Gipp replied unequivocally, 'What's tough about it?' "

With neither Gipp nor Rockne available for comment, presumably the truth will never be known.

Postscript: Just prior to a game against Notre Dame in the mid-fifties, Michigan State coach Duffy Daugherty approached one of his players, Clarence Peaks, and asked, "Clarence, you going to let the Gipper beat you this afternoon?"

"If he shows up," Peaks replied, "Exit 15 is mine."

CASEY STENGEL
major league manager:

"You could look it up."

Achieved "classic" status through sheer repetition by Stengel. The garrulous manager loved to punctuate his declarative sentences with this simple assertion. You could look it up.

SATCHEL PAIGE
Hall of Fame pitcher:

"Don't look back. Something might be gaining on you."

The sixth and last of Paige's Rules for Staying Young, which were first published in the old *Collier's* magazine. The rules were embroidered by writer Richard Donovan, who pieced them together from the pitcher's colorful conversation. The other rules:

Avoid fried meats, which angry up the blood.

If your stomach disputes you, lie down and pacify it with cool thoughts.

Keep the juices flowing by jangling around gently as you move.

Go very light on the vices, such as carrying on in society. The social ramble ain't restful.

Avoid running at all times.

JOE LOUIS
heavyweight boxing champion:

"He can run, but he can't hide."

Louis' response to those who kept reminding him of challenger Billy Conn's speed and hit-and-run tactics prior to the June, 1946 title match between the two fighters. Conn managed to run for seven rounds before the champion caught him in the eighth and knocked him out.

GRANTLAND RICE
sportswriter:

"Outlined against a blue-gray October sky, the Four Horsemen rode again. In dramatic lore they are known as Famine, Pestilence, Destruction and Death. These are only aliases. Their real names are Stuhldreher, Miller, Crowley and Layden."

Appeared in the New York *Herald-Tribune* on October 19, 1924, as the lead for Rice's report on the Notre Dame–Army football game, won by the Irish, 13–7. The "Four Horsemen" appellation immortalized the Notre Dame backfield of quarterback Harry Stuhldreher, halfbacks Don Miller and Jim Crowley, and fullback Elmer Layden.

Thirty years later, Miller reminisced with Rice. "Let's face it," Miller said. "We were good, sure. But we'd have been just as dead two years after graduation as any other backfield if you hadn't painted that tag line on us."

To be sure, Miller and the other Horsemen may owe their lasting fame to George Strickler, a student publicist for the Irish in 1924. Three days before the Army game, Strickler had seen the film version of Blasco Ibáñez's novel *Four Horsemen of the Apocalypse,* starring Rudolph Valentino. Seated near Rice in the press box on Saturday, Strickler watched the Notre Dame backfield attack Army. "Just like the Four Horsemen," he observed innocently.

Rice probably heard the remark, but in his recollection of the famous lead, set forth in his book *The Tumult and The Shouting,* he makes no mention of Strickler. In fact, he claims to have had the seed of the idea for the Four Horsemen nickname a year before he actually committed it to print. He had seen the 1923 Army–Notre Dame game at Ebbets Field; and, impressed with the Irish backfield, remarked to a companion, "It's worse than a cavalry charge. They're like a wild horse stampede."

Regardless of how the tag was conceived, its lasting celebrity was guaranteed the day after it was published by a classic photograph of the uniform-clad Four Horsemen on horseback. The picture—Strickler's idea—appeared in newspapers throughout the country.

JACK ROPER
heavyweight boxer:

"I zigged when I should have zagged."
Roper's explanation after champion Joe Louis knocked him out in the first round of their 1939 title bout in Los Angeles

MUHAMMAD ALI
heavyweight boxing champion:

"I am the greatest."
Ali's trademark boast, backed up by an illustrious ring career that saw him gain the world heavyweight championship an unprecedented three times.

"I just *said* I was the greatest," Ali admitted to a reporter from the Miami *News* late in his career. "I never thought I was.

"A long time ago I saw Gorgeous George promote a wrestling match he had coming up. He promised blood and guts. He promised to kill his opponent. He said anything to sell tickets. And he sold out.

"I saw an opportunity to do the same thing. So I started the 'I am the greatest' thing. I began with the poetry and predicting rounds. And it worked. They started coming in with their ten- and twenty-dollar bills to see the braggin' nigger.

"How do I know who the greatest fighter was? How can you compare fighters from different eras? I was probably the best of my time, but how do I know what would have happened if I fought Louis, Dempsey or Jack Johnson? I've been looking at some old boxing films, and some of those guys were tremendous."

BUD ABBOTT AND LOU COSTELLO
comedians:

"Who's on first, What's on second, I Don't Know is on third."

The most memorable line from Abbott and Costello's famous baseball routine, "Who's on First?" The comedians performed the now classic dialogue in burlesque shows in the thirties. They popularized it on CBS radio's *The Kate Smith Hour,* and immortalized it on Broadway in 1939.

In 1945, Abbott and Costello performed "Who's on First?" in their film *The Naughty Nineties* using one of endless variations on the routine. A typical version:

Who's on First?

Bud: You know, strange as it may seem, they give ballplayers peculiar names nowadays. On the St. Louis team Who's on first, What's on second, I Don't Know is on third.

Lou: That's what I want to find out. I want you to tell me the names of the fellows on the St. Louis team.

Bud: I'm telling you. Who's on first, What's on second, I Don't Know is on third.

Lou: You know the fellows' names?

Bud: Yes.

Lou: Well, then, who's playin' first?

Bud: Yes.

Lou: I mean the fellow's name on first base.

Bud: Who.

Lou: The fellow's name on first base for St. Louis.

Bud: Who.

Lou: The guy on first base.

Bud: Who is on first base.

Lou: Well, what are you askin' me for?

Bud: I'm not asking you, I'm telling you. Who is on first.

Lou: I'm askin' you, Who is on first?

Bud: That's the man's name.

Lou: That's whose name?

Bud: Yes.

Lou: Well, go ahead, tell me.

Bud: Who.

Lou: The guy on first.

Bud: Who.

Lou: The first baseman.

Bud: Who is on first.

Lou [a new approach]: Have you got a first baseman on first?

Bud: Certainly.

Lou: Well, all I'm trying' to find out is what's the guy's name on first base.

Bud: Oh, no, no. What is on second base.

Lou: I'm not askin' you who's on second.

Bud: Who's on first.

Lou: That's what I'm tryin' to find out.

Bud: Well, don't change the players around.

Lou [tension mounting]: I'm not changin' anybody.

Bud: Now take it easy.

Lou: What's the guy's name on first base?

Bud: What's the guy's name on *second* base.

Lou: I'm not askin' you who's on second.

Bud: Who's on first.

Lou: I don't know.

Bud: He's on third. We're not talking about him.

Lou [imploringly]: How could I get on third base?

Bud: You mentioned his name.

Lou: If I mentioned the third baseman's name, who did I say is playing third?

Bud [insistently]: No, Who's playing first.

Lou: Stay offa first, will ya?

Bud: Please, now what is it you'd like to know?

Lou: What is the fellow's name on third base?

Bud: What is the fellow's name on *second* base.

Lou: I'm not askin' ya who's on second.

Bud: Who's on first.

Lou: I don't know.

Bud and Lou in unison: Third base!

Lou [trying a new tack]: You got an outfield?

Bud: Certainly.

Lou: St. Louis got a good outfield?

Bud: Oh, absolutely.

Lou: The left fielder's name?

Bud: Why.

Lou: I don't know. I just thought I'd ask.

Bud: Well, I just thought I'd tell you.

Lou: Then tell me who's playing left field.

Bud: Who's playing first.

Lou: Stay outa the infield!

Bud: Don't mention any names out here.

Lou [firmly]: I wanta know what's the fellow's name in left field.

Bud: What is on second.

Lou: I'm not askin' you who's on second.

Bud: Who is on first.

Lou: I don't know!

Bud and Lou: Third base!

[Lou begins making noises.]

Bud: Now take it easy, man.

Lou: And the left fielder's name?

Bud: Why.

Lou: Because.

Bud: Oh, he's center field.

Lou: Wait a minute. You got a pitcher on the team?

Bud: Wouldn't this be a fine team without a pitcher?

Lou: I dunno. Tell me the pitcher's name.

Bud: Tomorrow.

Lou: You don't want to tell me today?

Bud: I'm telling you, man.

Lou: Then go ahead.

Bud: Tomorrow.

Lou: What time?

Bud: What time what?

Lou: What time tomorrow are you gonna tell me who's pitching?

Bud: Now listen, who is not pitching. Who is on—

Lou [excitedly]: I'll break your arm if you say who is on first!

Bud: Then why come up here and ask?

Lou: I want to know what's the pitcher's name!

Bud: What's on second.

Lou [resigned]: I don't know.

Bud and Lou: Third base.

Lou: You gotta catcher?

Bud: Yes.

Lou: The catcher's name.

Bud: Today.

Lou: Today. And Tomorrow's pitching.

Bud: Now you've got it.

Lou: That's all. St. Louis got a couple of days on their team. That's all.

Bud: Well, I can't help that. What do you want me to do?

Lou: Gotta catcher?

Bud: Yes.

Lou: I'm a good catcher, too, you know.

Bud: I know that.

Lou: I would like to play for St. Louis.

Bud: Well, I might arrange that.

Lou: I would like to catch. Now Tomorrow's pitching on the team and I'm catching.

Bud: Yes.

Lou: Tomorrow throws the ball and the guy up and bunts the ball.

Bud: Yes.

Lou: So when he bunts the ball, me, bein' a good catcher, I want to throw the guy out at first base. So I pick up the ball and throw it to who?

Bud: Now that's the first thing you've said right!

Lou: *I don't even know what I'm talking about!*

Bud: Well, that's all you have to do.

Lou: I throw it to first base.

Bud: Yes.

Lou: Now who's got it?

Bud: Naturally.

Lou: Who has it?

Bud: Naturally.

Lou: Naturally.

Bud: Naturally.

Lou: I throw the ball to naturally.

Bud: You throw it to Who.

Lou: Naturally.

Bud: Naturally, well, say it that way.

Lou: That's what I'm saying!

Bud: Now don't get excited, don't get excited.

Lou: I throw the ball to first base.

Bud: Then Who gets it.

Lou: He'd better get it!

Bud: That's it. All right now, don't get excited. Take it easy.

Lou [frenzied]: Now I throw the ball to first base, whoever it is grabs the ball, so the guy runs to second.

Bud: Uh-huh.

Lou: Who picks up the ball and throws it to What, What throws it to I Don't Know. I Don't Know throws it back to Tomorrow. A triple play!

Bud: Yeah, it could be.

Lou: Another guy gets up and it's a long fly ball to center. Why? I don't know. And I don't care.

Bud: What was that?

Lou: I said, I don't care.

Bud: Oh, that's our shortstop.

Coaches and Coaching

TOMMY PROTHRO
UCLA football coach:

"Coaching is an unnatural way of life. It's natural for me because I'm used to it, but it would be unnatural for most persons. Your victories and losses are too clear-cut."

BUM PHILLIPS
Houston Oilers coach:

"The main thing is getting people to *play*. When you think it's your system that's winning, you're in for a damn big surprise. It's those players' efforts."

WHITEY HERZOG
Kansas City Royals manager, on what it takes to be a success in his business:

"A sense of humor and a good bullpen."

BEAR BRYANT
Alabama football coach:

"I've never recommended anybody go into coaching, 'cause if they have enough on the ball, if they can do without coaching, they should do without it. If they put as much work into it and spend as much time, the rewards are going to be much better in something else."

ABE LEMONS
Texas basketball coach:

"I'm sure I'd rather be doing something else. You know what they call the guy who finishes last in medical school? They call him Doctor!"

BEAR BRYANT
Alabama football coach:

"Most coaches study the films when they lose. I study them when we win—to see if I can figure out what I did right."

LEO DUROCHER
Brooklyn Dodgers manager:

"You don't save a pitcher for tomorrow. Tomorrow it may rain."

PEPPER RODGERS
former Georgia Tech football coach, noting that he was fired the day after he had lunch with President Jimmy Carter:

"I'm the only coach in history to go straight from the White House to the outhouse."

DON CHERRY
former Colorado Rockies coach, on his firing:

"I am happy I wasn't around for the crucifixion, because I would have gotten blamed for that."

JOHN RALSTON
former Denver Broncos coach, explaining his departure from the team:

"I left because of illness and fatigue. The fans were sick and tired of me."

BEAR BRYANT
Alabama football coach, recalling his coaching days at Kentucky where he was overshadowed by basketball coach Adolph Rupp:

"I knew it was time to leave when they had a banquet and they gave Adolph a Cadillac and gave me a cigarette lighter."

DARRELL ROYAL
Texas football coach:

"I'm always thinking about the games we lost, not the ones we won."

AL CONOVER
after serving as Rice football coach:

"I'm going to become a hog farmer. After some of the things I've been through, I regard it as a step up."

BUD GRANT
Minnesota Vikings coach:

"There are coaches who spend 18 hours a day coaching the perfect game, and they lose because the ball is oval and they can't control the bounce."

CHUCK KNOX
Buffalo Bills coach:

"They say the breaks all even up in the long run. But how many of us last that long?"

C. W. NEWTON
Alabama basketball coach:

"When a coach is hired, he's fired. The date just hasn't been filled in yet."

BILLY MARTIN
major league manager, on when a manager should start looking for another job:

"When you arrive at the ball park and find your name has been scratched from the parking list."

FRED SHERO
professional hockey coach:

"You can't be happy coaching. If you're happy coaching, you should get out of the game. You've got to suffer. If you're happy all day long, you've got to be an idiot."

JOHNNY KERR
NBA player and coach-turned-sportscaster:

"Who needs five guys running around out on the court with your paycheck?"

CASEY STENGEL
Brooklyn Dodgers manager:

"It's like I used to tell my barber. Shave and a haircut, but don't cut my throat. I may want to do that myself."

JOE PATERNO
Penn State athletic director and football coach:

"The minute you think you've got it made, disaster is just around the corner."

AMOS ALONZO STAGG
college football coach:

"No coach ever won a game by what he knows; it's what his players have learned."

DARRELL ROYAL
Texas football coach:

"A coach isn't as smart as they say he is when he wins, or as stupid when he loses."

JOHNNY KERR
NBA player and coach-turned-sportscaster:

"If a coach starts listening to the fans, he winds up sitting next to them."

GABE PAUL
Cleveland Indians president:

"A manager really gets paid for how much he suffers."

CASEY STENGEL
major league manager:

"The secret of managing a club is to keep the five guys who hate you away from the five who are undecided."

BILLY MARTIN
New York Yankees manager:

"Out of 25 guys there should be 15 who would run through a wall for you, two or three who don't like you at all, five who are indifferent and maybe three undecided. My job is to keep the last two groups from going the wrong way."

TOMMY LASORDA
Los Angeles Dodgers manager:

"Managing is like holding a dove in your hand. Squeeze too hard and you kill it; not hard enough and it flies away."

BIRDIE TEBBETTS
former major league manager:

"Managing a ball club is a job for which a man works, studies, hopes and, if he's gaited that way, prays—knowing all the time that if he gets it, he's bound, in the end, to be fired."

JOE KAPP
former NFL quarterback, on being named football coach at California despite having no previous coaching experience:

"Howard Cosell coaches 28 NFL teams every week, so I figure I can coach one college team."

BILL VAN BREDA KOLFF
former NBA coach, on why he preferred coaching the New Orleans Pride of the Women's Basketball League:

"The time-outs smell a lot better."

JIM FREY
Kansas City Royals manager, revealing the advice he gives George Brett about hitting:

"I tell him, 'Attaway to hit, George.' "

LOU HOLTZ
Arkansas football coach, on why he prefers a squatting posture on the sidelines during games:

"It makes a tougher target for the fans to hit."

JOHNNY CARSON
The *Tonight* show host:

"There are close to 11 million unemployed, and half of them are New York Yankee managers."

ABE LEMONS
basketball coach, just fired from his job at the University of Texas, describing his reaction when athletic director DeLoss Dodds gave him the news:

"I looked around the room and nobody else was there, so he had to be talking to me."

CASEY STENGEL
New York Yankees manager, pointing toward the stands as he explained to a pitcher why he had to pull him from the game:

"Up there people are beginning to talk."

GENE MAUCH
major league manager:

"The worst thing about managing is the day you realize you want to win more than the players do."

JIM FREGOSI
California Angels manager, advising a rookie manager:

"Get yourself a coach to drink with or else you'll go nuts."

JIM MCGREGOR
basketball coach, on the advantages of coaching abroad:

"If you see an NCAA investigator, you know he is on vacation."

PEE WEE REESE
former Brooklyn Dodgers shortstop, on making the transition from player to coach:

"I felt like a mosquito in a nudist colony. I didn't know where to begin."

BUM PHILLIPS
Houston Oilers coach:

"There are two types of coaches. Them that have just been fired and them that are going to be fired."

WREN BLAIR
Pittsburgh Penguins president, asked if one of his appointees was an interim coach:

"Aren't all coaches interim coaches?"

LOU HOLTZ
Arkansas football coach:

"When I go home at night, I'm just thankful to get through another day without a mutiny."

JOHN MCKAY
Tampa Bay Buccaneers coach:

"A genius in the National Football League is a guy who won last week."

AL MCGUIRE
Marquette basketball coach-turned-sportscaster:

"Coaches think everybody is talking about them. They don't realize they're just a coffee break. The only time people at Equitable Life or Sperry Rand talk about them is when they're eating Danish. They all have their own problems."

BUM PHILLIPS
Houston Oilers Coach:

"The trouble with most coaches is they start with the assumption that everybody is a turd. And that ain't right."

JIM MURRAY
sportswriter:

"If you scratch the average football coach, you will find William McKinley underneath. Some of them come to work on stone wheels."

EMMETT WATSON
writer:

"Football coaches are a class of selfless sufferers who go on building character year after year, no matter how many states they have to import it from."

TORCHY CLARK
Florida Tech basketball coach, on NCAA Division II coaches:

"We get less publicity. We get less money. But we are equal in getting high blood pressure, ulcers, heart attacks and, oh yes, fired."

EMMETT WATSON
writer:

"Don't raise your boy to be a football coach. In fact, be more cautious than that. At the first sign of his desire to become a football coach, just stop raising him."

DIZZY DEAN
Hall of Fame pitcher, summarizing his belief that the manager has baseball's easiest job:

"There's *one* guy who should pay to get into the park."

ALOIS BLACKWELL
Houston University football recruit, on why he elected to play for Veer-T innovator Bill Yeoman:

"Why take a piece of cake from just anybody when you can get one from Betty Crocker?"

CASEY STENGEL
baseball manager, on the advantage of becoming manager of the minor league Acorns in Oakland, California at age 56:

"Every manager wants to jump off a bridge sooner or later, and it is very nice for an old man like me to know he don't have to walk 50 miles to find one."

DON ZIMMER
Boston Red Sox manager, on why he habitually arrived for games several hours early:

"I want to make sure nobody's in my uniform."

CHUCK ESTRADA
Texas Rangers pitching coach, on how he decides which relief pitcher to use:

"Whoever answers the bullpen phone."

JACK LORRI
sportscaster, on how he knew Notre Dame was having trouble selecting a new football coach after Dan Devine's departure:

"When I looked up at the Golden Dome, the two puffs of smoke coming out of the top were black."

ALEX HAWKINS
broadcaster:

"I'd rather listen to a bad minister than to a coach talk about football."

CHUCK NOLL
Pittsburgh Steelers coach:

"A life of frustration is inevitable for any coach whose main enjoyment is winning."

JIM CROWLEY
Notre Dame halfback, responding to coach Knute Rockne's question, "It's our ball on the enemy's two-yardline, fourth down, goal to go. What would you do?":

"I'd move over on the bench a little so I could see the touchdown better."

BRUCE OGILVIE
sports psychologist:

"When you are discussing a successful coach, you are not necessarily drawing the profile of an entirely healthy person."

WELLINGTON MARA
New York Giants owner, on football coaches:

"Few die on the job."

FRED AKERS
Texas football coach:

"Football doesn't take me away from my family life. We've always watched films together."

ABE LEMONS
Texas basketball coach, on why he keeps his coaching strategies simple:

"You could tell five guys to go over to the post office at 2 o'clock and one of 'em wouldn't be there, so why have so many tricky plays?"

LOU HOLTZ
Arkansas football coach:

"I don't mind starting a season with unknowns. I just don't like finishing a season with a bunch of them."

DOUG DICKEY
Florida football coach, on why losing three games in a season is better than losing just one:

"The fans talk about the games you won following a 7–3 season. When you go 9–1 they talk about the one you lost."

WOODY HAYES
Ohio State football coach, on why he never praises opponents:

"If I build up another team, they are liable to believe me."

BARRY SWITZER
Oklahoma football coach:

"I've always said that if I had my way, I'd like to be undefeated and unimpressive."

ABE LEMONS
Texas basketball coach, on why he doesn't compel his players to attend practices—or games, for that matter:

"If one sumbitch don't show up, we'll play another sumbitch."

DEAN SMITH
North Carolina basketball coach:

"If you make every game a life-and-death proposition, you're going to have problems. For one thing, you'll be dead a lot."

DARRELL ROYAL
Texas football coach:

"Winning coaches must treat mistakes like copperheads in the bedclothes—avoid them with all the energy you can muster."

HANK STRAM
former NFL coach:

"When I got into the coaching business, I knew I was getting into a high-risk, high-profile profession, so I adopted a philosophy I've never wavered from. Yesterday is a canceled check, today is cash on the line, tomorrow is a promissory note."

LOU HOLTZ
Arkansas football coach:

"Don't ever ask a player to do something he doesn't have the ability to do, because he'll question your ability as a coach, not his as an athlete."

JIM MURRAY
sportswriter, on football coaches:

"Coaches spend fortunes cataloging the habits of opponents because football teams, like whooping cranes or spawning salmon and other migratory creatures like the Pacific gray whale, do the same thing in the same way over and over again, generation after generation.

"All teams, for example, run off tackle on first down, pass on third down, and punt on fourth. And whales mate in Magdalena Bay or Scammons Lagoon. And birds go south in the winter. And moss grows on the north side of trees."

GENE MAUCH
Montreal Expos manager:

"I'm not the manager because I'm always right, but I'm always right because I'm the manager."

RED SANDERS
UCLA football coach, in an aside to his wife when a cheering horde of students serenaded his apartment and begged him not to accept an offer to coach at Florida:

"Which one has the rope?"

KNUTE ROCKNE
Notre Dame football coach, upon poking his head inside the door of the locker room after his team had been mauled in the first half of a game:

"Oh, excuse me, ladies! I thought this was the Notre Dame team."

WILL ROGERS
humorist:

"Successful colleges will start laying plans for a new stadium; unsuccessful ones will start hunting for a new coach."

LOU HOLTZ
New York Jets coach, shortly after taking the job:

"We're building a house on Long Island. We're optimistic. It's a little like doing a crossword puzzle with a pen."

GEORGE ALLEN
Washington Redskins coach:

"Nobody should work all the time. Everyone should have some leisure, but I believe the early morning hours are best for this —the five or six hours when you're asleep."

PAPPY WALDORF
California football coach:

"Good players win games for you, not big players."

JOHN WOODEN
UCLA basketball coach:

"It's what you learn after you know it all that counts."
   (Also attributed to professional hockey coach Fred Shero)

ABE LEMONS
Pan American College basketball coach:

"I'd rather be a football coach. That way you can lose only 11 games a season. I lost 11 games in December alone."

HARRY NEALE
Vancouver Canucks coach:

"Last season we couldn't win at home and we were losing on the road. My failure as a coach was that I couldn't think of anyplace else to play."

TOMMY LASORDA
Los Angeles Dodgers manager:

"I found out that it's not good to talk about my troubles. Eighty percent of the people who hear them don't care and the other 20 percent are glad you're having trouble."

DARRELL JOHNSON
Seattle Mariners manager, on how he knows when to make a pitching change:

"You just listen to the bat and ball come together. They make an awful noise."

LOU HOLTZ
Arkansas football coach, dismissing rumors he would leave Arkansas to coach at South Carolina:

"I have never thought of leaving Arkansas since I got here. Suicide yes, leaving no."

BEAR BRYANT
Alabama football coach and early riser, on whether it's true he can walk on water:

"Well, I won't say I can or I can't; but if I do, I do it before most people get up in the morning."

WOODY HAYES
Ohio State football coach:

"I had a Cadillac offered to me a couple of times. You know how that works. They give you the Cadillac one year, and the next year they give you the gas to get out of town."

BILL RUSSELL
former Seattle SuperSonics coach, on why he had difficulty coaching some of his players:

"I tried to treat them like me—and some of them weren't."

JOHN MCKAY
University of Southern California football coach:

"As soon as a coach begs, 'Please, please play for me,' he becomes a whore. Don't play hard for me. Play hard for yourself. If you don't want to, fine. But if we lose, don't come sobbing to me."

LOU HOLTZ
Arkansas football coach, on the close public scrutiny he endures:

"Being head coach at Arkansas is like being a state park."

BUD GRANT
Minnesota Vikings coach:

"A good coach needs a patient wife, loyal dog and a great quarterback—not necessarily in that order."

DALE BANDY
Ohio University basketball coach, on being a head coach after having served as an assistant:

"I never realized there was such a difference between making a suggestion and making a decision."

BOB GRIESE
former Miami Dolphins quarterback, upon leaving the Dolphins coaching staff to enter private business:

"If you want to drop off the face of the earth, just be an assistant coach."

BEAR BRYANT
Alabama football coach, reflecting on his career:

"I ain't never had much fun. I ain't never been two inches away from a football. Here guys go fishing on the day of the game, hunting, golfing, and all I want to do is be alone, studying how not to lose."

LOU HOLTZ
Arkansas football coach:

"Coaching is nothing more than eliminating mistakes before you get fired."

CHARLIE PELL
Clemson football coach:

"I demand just one thing from Clemson players, and that is attitude. I want them to think as positively as the 85-year-old man who married a 25-year-old woman and ordered a five-bedroom house near an elementary school."

FRED SHERO
professional hockey coach:

"When you're a coach, you're miserable. When you're not a coach, you're more miserable."

RED AUERBACH
Boston Celtics coach:

"I have two college degrees, but I know nothing except how to help guys put a ball in a hole."

JIM MURRAY
sportswriter, on former Cleveland Browns coach Paul Brown:

"A man of glacial contempt, spare and fussy, he treated his players as if he had bought them at auction with a ring in their noses and was trying not to notice they smelled bad."

DON MEREDITH
former Dallas Cowboys quarterback, on Cowboys coach Tom Landry:

"He's a perfectionist. If he was married to Raquel Welch, he'd expect her to cook."

WALT GARRISON
former Dallas Cowboys fullback, asked if Cowboys coach Tom Landry ever smiles:

"I don't know. I only played there nine years."

TOM LANDRY
Dallas Cowboys coach, reminded in 1981 that he was the only head coach in the team's history:

"That's one way to look at it. The other is that I haven't had a promotion in 21 years."

JOHN MCKAY
Tampa Bay Buccaneers coach, on his mail:

"It's about three to one that I'm not an s.o.b. But there are a lot of ones."

JOE MORGAN
San Francisco Giants second baseman, on manager Frank Robinson's diplomatic manner of issuing constructive criticism:

"He can step on your shoes, but he doesn't mess up your shine."

HENRY JORDAN
Green Bay Packers defensive lineman, on coach Vince Lombardi:

"Lombardi treats us all the same—like dogs."

LOU HOLTZ
Arkansas football coach, acknowledging his reliance on his assistants:

"According to the Bible, Joseph died leaning on his staff, and I think the same will be said of me."

BUM PHILLIPS
Houston Oilers coach, on the demands for loyalty he places on his players:

"I can get away with all this because they like me. If they didn't, the sonsabitches would kill me."

BILL FITCH
Boston Celtics coach:

"I don't have an ulcer. I'm a carrier. I give them to other people."

BILL WALTON
Portland Trail Blazers center, on the supreme confidence of coach Jack Ramsay:

"If he's behind eight points with ten seconds to play, Jack is there on the bench figuring out a nine-point play."

WARREN SPAHN
Hall of Fame pitcher who played under manager Casey Stengel with the 1942 Boston Braves and the 1965 New York Mets:

"I'm probably the only guy who worked for Stengel before and after he was a genius."

JIMMIE DYKES
Cleveland Indians manager, asked to identify Casey Stengel's greatest managerial asset:

"He's independently wealthy."

ROCKY BLEIER
Pittsburgh Steelers running back, on the extraordinary self-assurance of Steelers coach Chuck Noll:

"He's the only person I know who bought a plane before he learned to fly."

PEPPER RODGERS
college football coach:

"I want this on my tombstone: 'Pepper Rodgers was a terrible recruiter, but he overcame it with great coaching.'"

Concentration

RON LAIRD
U.S. race walker, after going off course in the Pan-American Games 20,000-meter walk:

"I knew something was wrong when I came to a locked gate."

BOBBY NICHOLS
professional golfer:

"If you've got to remind yourself to concentrate during competition, you've got no chance to concentrate."

CARMEN BASILIO
former welterweight boxing champion:

"I can't concentrate on golf or bowling. I could concentrate in the ring because someone was trying to kill me. Those bowling pins aren't going to hurt me."

BRANCH RICKEY
St. Louis Cardinals general manager:

"A full mind is an empty bat."

Confidence

JOE PATERNO
Penn State football coach:

"Besides pride, loyalty, discipline, heart and mind, confidence is the key to all the locks."

STAN SMITH
professional tennis player:

"Experience tells you what to do; confidence allows you to do it."

JOHN MCKAY
University of Southern California football coach:

"When I went duck hunting with Bear Bryant, he shot at one but it kept flying. 'John,' he said, 'there flies a dead duck.' Now *that's* confidence."

Contracts and Salaries

AL MCGUIRE
Marquette basketball
coach-turned-sportscaster:

"I think an agent should get
paid by the hour. I don't
believe anyone should own a
percentage of anyone else.
That's one of the reasons we
fought the Civil War."

BILL VEECK
Chicago White Sox owner, asked
whether free agents lean toward
playing in big cities:

"Not really. They lean toward
cash."

BILL VEECK
Chicago White Sox owner:

"It isn't really the stars that are expensive. It's the high cost of
mediocrity."

ART ROONEY
Pittsburgh Steelers owner:

"You can never overpay a good player. You can only overpay
a bad one. I don't mind paying a good player $200,000. What
I mind is paying a $20,000 ballplayer $22,000."

MICKEY MANTLE
Hall of Fame outfielder, in 1979, on the escalation of player salaries since his
retirement:

"I measure it by Cadillacs. I used to pay $5,000 for mine. They
pay $20,000 now. So, if they make three times as much as I did,
what's the difference?"

KEN HOLTZMAN
major league pitcher, on his contract negotiations with the Chicago Cubs in
1968:

"We're still about two Cadillacs apart."

CLIFF PARSLEY
Houston Oilers punter, on kicking specialists' earnings:

"People think our income is much greater than it really is. I'm
barely making enough to pay off my Cadillac."

ZOLLIE VOLCHOK
Seattle SuperSonics general manager, in 1979:

"Today's salaries are way out of line. If they continue to escalate
like they are, the only people who will be able to afford to buy
tickets will be the players and their agents."

BILL RUSSELL
former Boston Celtics center, asked how much CBS was paying him to do commentary on NBA games:

"As the Rolls-Royce said when the Aston-Martin asked him how much horsepower he had: 'Sufficient.'"

STEVE STONE
Baltimore Orioles pitcher:

"I don't think Johnny Carson got a lot of hate mail when he signed for $5 million. But Bruce Sutter probably did. Why? Well, Johnny's a lot funnier than Bruce. I mean, Bruce is a wonderful guy, but his Karnak is weak."

DENNY CRUM
Louisville basketball coach:

"I'm getting $300,000 but over a 150-year period."

PETE ROSE
Philadelphia Phillies first baseman, at age 39:

"With all the money I make now, I don't get my uniform any less dirty than when I was nine years old. The only difference is that my mother used to wash it."

BILL VEECK
Chicago White Sox owner:

"We will scheme, connive, steal and do everything possible to win the pennant—except pay big salaries."

GREG BUTTLE
New York Jets linebacker:

"They pay me to practice during the week. On Sunday I play for nothing."

DOUG CAMILLI
Los Angeles Dodgers catcher, after traveling back and forth between the minors and the majors for two seasons:

"In my new contract I'm going to ask the Dodgers to pay me by the mile."

JIM KERN
Texas Rangers pitcher:

"Isn't it amazing that we're worth so much on the trading block and worth so little when we talk salary with the general manager?"

BILLY LOES
Brooklyn Dodgers pitcher, in response to general manager Branch Rickey, who had requested that Loes keep secret the terms of the contract he had just signed:

"Don't worry. I'm just as ashamed of the figures as you are."

JOE PATERNO
Penn State football coach, after turning down a million-dollar offer to coach the New England Patriots:

"What the hell's the matter with a society that offers a football coach a million dollars?"

JOE DIMAGGIO
New York Yankees outfielder, on why he refused his last Yankee contract:

"I didn't think I could give them a hundred-thousand-dollar year."

NOLAN RYAN
California Angels pitcher, on why he didn't ask for a salary increase during the 1973 season when he pitched two no-hitters and almost pitched a third one:

"They didn't try to cut my pay when I was going bad, did they?"

BLACKIE SHERROD
sportswriter, on a complaint by Atlanta Braves owner Ted Turner that baseball salaries are too high:

"That's like Al Capone speaking out for gun control."

MIKE NORRIS
Oakland A's pitcher, accepting an arbitration award of $325,000 instead of the $450,000 he had sought:

"No problem. I was either going to wake up rich or richer."

BOB DEVANEY
Nebraska football coach, on why he didn't seek a lifetime contract:

"I had a friend with a lifetime contract. After two bad years, the university president called him into his office and pronounced him dead."

HAYDEN FRY
Iowa football coach:

"I thought I had a lifetime contract. Then I found out the other day that if I have a losing season they're going to declare me legally dead."

LOU HOLTZ
Arkansas football coach:

"I have a lifetime contract. That means I can't be fired during the third quarter if we're ahead and moving the ball."

BABE RUTH
Hall of Fame outfielder, when told that President Hoover made less than the $80,000 Ruth was demanding in 1930:

"I had a better year than he did."

(Red Smith, sportswriter: "[Ruth's salary] was more than President Herbert Hoover received, but if this was ever pointed out to Ruth he almost surely did not reply, as the story goes: 'I had a better year than he did.' He would have been correct, but the Babe was not that well informed on national affairs.")

DAVE WILLIAMS
Houston golf coach, suggesting one-year scholarships instead of the standard four-year agreements:

"The only person I know working on a four-year contract is the President of the United States—and he can get impeached."

RED GRANGE
former Illinois and Chicago Bears running back:

"No player is worth a million dollars. I can understand why a player would have an agent. I couldn't keep from laughing if I went in and demanded a million dollars from an owner."

DUKE SNIDER
former Brooklyn/Los Angeles Dodgers outfielder:

"Man, if I made a million dollars I would come in at six in the morning, sweep the stands, wash the uniforms, clean out the offices, manage the team and play the game."

DAVE WINFIELD
San Diego Padres outfielder, on the hostility directed toward him once it became known he was asking for $2 million a year:

"I think most of the booing is coming from the owners' boxes."

TUG MCGRAW
major league relief pitcher, on how he intended to budget his salary increase:

"Ninety percent I'll spend on good times, women and Irish whiskey. The other 10 percent I'll probably waste."

ED BADGER
Cincinnati basketball coach, on why he prefers coaching in college to the NBA:

"In college, when I call a time-out, at least I know I'm the highest-paid guy in the huddle."

BOB FELLER
Hall of Fame pitcher:

"I was a bonus baby. I got two autographed baseballs and a scorecard from the 1935 All-Star game."

BOB UECKER
sportscaster, recalling when he signed with the Milwaukee Braves for $3,000:

"That bothered my dad at the time, because he didn't have that kind of dough to pay out. But eventually he scraped it up."

PAT GILLICK
Toronto Blue Jays executive, on the demand of 39-year-old free agent Rico Carty for a three-year contract:

"I don't mind paying a player, but I don't want to pay for his funeral."

PETE ROSE
Philadelphia Phillies first baseman:

"With the money I'm making, I should be playing two positions."

Courage

ANONYMOUS BULLFIGHTER:

"To fight a bull when you are not scared is nothing. And to not fight a bull when you are scared is nothing. But to fight a bull when you are scared—that is something."

EARL WILSON
entertainment writer:

"My idea of courage is the guy who has $500,000 tied up in the stock market and turns to the box scores first."

Death

BUM PHILLIPS
professional football coach:

"If I drop dead tomorrow, at least I'll know I died in good health."

WILLIE PEP
former featherweight boxing champion, on a report that he had died:

"Naw, I didn't die last night. I wasn't even out of the house."

BOBBY LAYNE
former Detroit Lions quarterback:

"My only request is that I draw my last dollar and my last breath at precisely the same instant."

JACK LALANNE
physical fitness tycoon, on why he doesn't intend to die:

"It would wreck my image. I can't even afford to have a fat dog."

TOM SNEVA
race driver:

"You just have to treat death like any other part of life."

DOROTHY SHULA
wife of Miami Dolphins coach Don Shula:

"I'm fairly confident that if I died tomorrow, Don would find a way to preserve me until the season was over and he had time for a nice funeral."

JOE LOUIS
former heavyweight boxing champion:

"Everybody wants to go to heaven, but nobody wants to die."
  (Eddie Donovan, New York Knicks general manager: "A lot of people want to go to heaven, but not too many people want to die to go there.")

BILL LEE
major league pitcher:

"I believe you come back as whatever you've abused in the previous life. If you're a dope smoker, you might come back as a tree and get processed into a Zig Zag or something. . . .

"I hope to come back as a grain in the field and get turned into some of the finest Dortmunder Union beer in Germany. And that Pelé will drink me."

Dedication

LOU HOLTZ
Arkansas football coach:

"If you don't make a total commitment to whatever you're doing, then you start looking to bail out the first time the boat starts leaking. It's tough enough getting that boat to shore with everybody rowing, let alone when a guy stands up and starts putting his life jacket on."

PAUL GALLICO
sportswriter:

"A 100 percent concern with a game to the exclusion of all else is surely tinged with obsession. The single-mindedness necessary to fight one's way to the top, in no matter what sport, is something not shared by the majority of mortals."

RON SWOBODA
major league outfielder:

"Why am I wasting so much dedication on a mediocre career?"

FILBERT BAYI
Tanzanian runner:

"World records are like shirts. Anyone can have one if he works for it."

Discipline

BUM PHILLIPS
Houston Oilers coach:

"The only discipline that lasts is self-discipline."

BOBBY BOWDEN
Florida State football coach, asked if discipline was the key to winning:

"If it was, Army and Navy would be playing for the national championship every year."

BUM PHILLIPS
Houston Oilers coach:

"My idea of discipline is not makin' guys do something, it's gettin' 'em to do it. There's a difference in bitchin' and coachin'."

Disposition

DARRELL ROYAL
Texas football coach:

"Only angry people win football games."

PAUL GALLICO
sportswriter:

"Cruelty and absolute lack of mercy are essential qualities in every successful prizefighter."

DEREK SANDERSON
Boston Bruins hockey player:

"A hockey player must have three things planted in his head: hate, greed and jealousy. He must hate the other guy, he must be greedy for the puck and he must be jealous when he loses."

JOHN MCKAY
University of Southern California football coach:

"Does a team have to be emotional to win? Well, I've always said nobody is more emotional than [my wife] Corky, and she can't play football worth a damn."

SAM HUFF
Hall of Fame linebacker, on the pro football psyche:

"It gets easier to be mean every year, and harder to get out of it at the end of the season. Pretty soon, there's no in-between. You're mean all year round. That's when you've been in pro football too long."

BEAR BRYANT
Alabama football coach, on the three types of individuals who play the game:

"First, there are those who are winners and know they are winners. Then, there are the losers who know they are losers. Then, there are those who are not winners but don't know it. They're the ones for me. They never quit trying. They're the soul of our game."

CHRIS EVERT LLOYD
professional tennis player:

"Everybody thinks I'm so controlled on court, but every night I'm crying, whether I'm watching a romantic movie or *Barnaby Jones.*"

BEN TEMPLETON
"The Sporting Life" cartoonist, on his symbiotic relationship with partner Tom Forman:

"Tom's manic and I'm depressive, and together we make one healthy person."

WOODY HAYES
Ohio State football coach:

"It worries me that there's supposed to be two coaches meaner than I am. I would hate to have them start referring to me as 'Good Old Woody.' "

VIN SCULLY
sportscaster, on Los Angeles Dodgers pitcher Burt Hooton:

"He's such a quiet person that the night the Dodgers won the World Series he went out and painted the town beige."

DONALD DAVIDSON
Houston Astros executive, on pitcher Joe Niekro's ability to relax:

"It takes him an hour and a half to watch *60 Minutes.*"

FRED SHERO
Philadelphia Flyers coach:

"I'm like a duck: calm above water, but paddling like hell underneath."

Divine Intervention

WILBUR EVANS
Southwest Conference publicist, on Texas baseball coach and former major leaguer Bibb Falk:

"Bibb is so dedicated to baseball that until a week or so ago he thought the first verse in the Bible said, 'In the big inning, God created heaven and earth.' "

BARBARA BARROW
professional golfer, after scoring five birdies on the final nine holes of a tournament to earn her first LPGA victory:

"God knew I couldn't putt, so He put me closer to the hole."

RICK TELANDER
sportswriter, on Notre Dame University:

"How can you really like a school that has 300-pound linemen and God on its side?"

JUDGE KENESAW MOUNTAIN LANDIS
major league baseball commissioner, upon learning that a light failure at Milwaukee's Borchert Field just as the home team was about to fall behind had been explained as "an act of God":

"There will be no more acts of God."

BILLY GRAHAM
Christian evangelist:

"More than being concerned with who's going to win the Super Bowl, I feel the Lord is probably more concerned that they might find a day other than Sunday to play it on."

LORD STORMONT M.S. MANCROFT
English politician:

"The British have never been a spiritually minded people, so they invented cricket to give them some notion of eternity."

BILL VEECK
major league baseball owner, summarizing his religious views:

"I believe in God, but I'm not too clear on the other details."

STEVE ECCLESTONE
Xavier (Ohio) University fullback from Canada, watching his first major league baseball game:

"What are those four priests doing out on the field?"

Drinking

BUD WILKINSON
Oklahoma football coach-turned-sportscaster:

"Drinking a beer won't hurt a player physically. But it is a chink in his moral armor."

KNUTE ROCKNE
Notre Dame football coach:

"Drink the first. Sip the second slowly. Skip the third."

DEAN MARTIN
entertainer:

"If you drink, don't drive. Don't even putt."

JIM BROSNAN
major league pitcher-turned-writer:

"Drinking is not a spectator sport."

JOHNNY BLOOD
former professional football running back and coach, on why he quit drinking:

"I thought I saw King Arthur's court and walked through a plate glass window to get there."

BOB LEMON
major league manager, on his days as a pitcher for the Cleveland Indians:

"I had my bad days on the field, but I didn't take them home with me. I left them in a bar along the way."

PAUL WANER
major league outfielder, on how he managed to hit successfully after drinking sprees:

"I see three baseballs, but I only swing at the middle one."

JOHN LARDNER
writer, on the alleged hiring of detectives by New York Yankees manager
Bucky Harris to tail some of his players:

"The Yankees should have been easy to stalk because, belonging to a high-class ball club, they drank martinis and left a trail of olives."

HERSCHEL WALKER
Georgia running back and teetotaler, asked why he wasn't even curious about
taking a drink:

"I'm curious about jumping off a cliff and I don't do that either."

RUBEN OLIVERAS
professional boxer, asked if he ever drank:

"Only when I'm drunk."

RABBIT MARANVILLE
major league infielder:

"There is much less drinking now than there was before 1927, because I quit drinking on May 24, 1927."

GUMP WORSLEY
Minnesota North Stars goalie, disputing an allegation that he did all his training
in St. Paul bars:

"That's not true. I've switched to Minneapolis now."

JOHN MOONEY
sportswriter:

"If your doctor warns that you have to watch your drinking, find a bar with a mirror."

BOBBY SHEEHAN
Colorado Rockies hockey player, claiming stories of his past drinking were
greatly exaggerated:

"It wasn't that I drank so much, it's just that I put it into such a small body."

TOOTS SHOR
restaurateur:

"Through booze I met two Chief Justices, 50 world champs, six Presidents, and DiMaggio and Babe Ruth."

Durability

BILL RUSSELL
former Boston Celtics center:

"Durability is part of what makes a great athlete."

KAREEM ABDUL-JABBAR
Los Angeles Lakers center, on the physical abuse he takes from opponents:

"Sometimes I think they think I'm a Timex watch. I hope I can keep on ticking."

MICKEY MANTLE
Hall of Fame outfielder, on Billy Martin and Whitey Ford, his nightlife pals with the New York Yankees:

"If I hadn't met those two at the start of my career, I would have lasted another five years."

JOHNNY BENCH
Cincinnati Reds catcher who converted to third base:

"A catcher and his body are like the outlaw and his horse. He's got to ride that nag till it drops."

Eating

ARCHIE MOORE
former light-heavyweight boxing champion:

"I am not a glutton, but I am an explorer of food."

DIZZY DEAN
Hall of Fame pitcher, asked by President Dwight D. Eisenhower during a round of golf how he could allow himself to become so overweight:

"Mr. President, I was on a diet for 25 years. Now that I'm makin' some money, I'm makin' sure I eat enough to make up for the lean years."

NICK SEITZ
writer:

"The breakfast of champions is not cereal, it's your opposition."

JIMMY CANNON
sportswriter:

"Ballplayers who are first into the dining room are usually last in the averages."

WAITE HOYT
New York Yankees pitcher, on Babe Ruth:

"If you cut that big slob in half, most of the concessions at Yankee Stadium would come pouring out."

JIM MURRAY
sportswriter:

"Babe Ruth, of course, was the all-time trencherman. His stomach used to rumble in the outfield if the other team had a big inning."

AL MCGUIRE
Marquette basketball coach-turned-sportscaster:

"When you go into a restaurant and the waitresses' ankles are dirty, you know the chili's good."

LEE CORSO
Indiana football coach, on the frequency of chicken dinners on the postseason banquet circuit:

"I no longer sleep. I roost."

JIM BAKKEN
former St. Louis Cardinals placekicker, on 280-pound Cardinals guard Bob Young:

"For his salad, you just pour vinegar and oil on your lawn and let him graze."

RALPH KINER
baseball broadcaster, on why Dick Allen would never appear on his postgame show:

"He said if he came on, all the cold cuts would be gone when he got back to the locker room."

CHARLEY HANNAH
Tampa Bay Buccaneers tackle, on dining with prodigious eater Abe Gibron:

"He was eating things we wouldn't even go swimming with in Alabama."

ART DONOVAN
former 310-pound Baltimore Colts defensive lineman, claiming he's a light eater:

"As soon as it's light, I start to eat."

DON MANOUKIAN
Oakland Raiders guard, ordering a steak:

"Just knock the breath out of it."

JOHN CANDELARIA
Pittsburgh Pirates pitcher, to Dave Parker when the portly Pirate outfielder told Candelaria he was a vegetarian:

"What do you eat, redwoods?"

WOODY ALLEN
comedian, on what it's like to dine with Howard Cosell:

"He broadcasts the meal."

Excuses

MIKE REID
Cincinnati Bengals defensive lineman:

"There are a thousand reasons for failure, but not a single excuse."

CHRISTY MATHEWSON
Hall of Fame pitcher:

"You must have an alibi to show why you lost. If you haven't one, you must fake one. Your self-confidence must be maintained. Always have that alibi. But keep it to yourself. That's where it belongs."

BENJAMIN FRANKLIN
statesman/scientist/philosopher on making excuses for losing:

"He who shelters himself under such untruths in trifling matters is no very sturdy moralist in things of greater consequence, where his fame and honour are at stake."

STANLEY WOODWARD
sportswriter, on coach Red Blaik's claim that his Army team might have fared better against Michigan had Army's center given the football a quarter turn before snapping it:

"That's like blaming the Johnstown flood on a leaky faucet in Altoona."

BUSTER BRANNON
Texas Christian University basketball coach:

"Don't be in any hurry to build a new gym. That way you lose your alibi."

MILLER HUGGINS
New York Yankees manager, on what a player needs while in a slump:

"A string of alibis."

LOU HOLTZ
Arkansas football coach:

"The man who complains about the way the ball bounces is likely the one who dropped it."

Executives

JOHNNY KERR
Phoenix Suns coach, on why he accepted an offer to coach the expansion franchise instead of moving into the Chicago Bulls front office:

"I've seen enough guys who were kicked upstairs and then found out they were working in a one-story building."

BOB ZUPPKE
Illinois football coach:

"No athletic director holds office longer than two unsuccessful football coaches."

VINCE LOMBARDI
Green Bay Packers coach and general manager:

"A real executive goes around with a worried look on his assistants."

Exercise

BENJAMIN FRANKLIN
statesman/scientist/philosopher:

"There is more exercise in one mile's riding on horseback than in five in a coach."

GEORGE SANTAYANA
philosopher:

"The need of exercise is a modern superstition, invented by people who ate too much and had nothing to think about. Athletics don't make anybody either long-lived or useful."

NORMAN MAILER
writer:

"Any workout which does not involve a certain minimum of danger or responsibility does not improve the body—it just wears it out."

SAMUEL JOHNSON
English critic:

"How much happiness is gained, and how much misery escaped, by frequent and violent agitation of the body."

BILL VAUGHAN
writer:

"As a nation we are dedicated to keeping physically fit—and parking as close to the stadium as possible."

MARK TWAIN
writer:

"Exercise is loathsome."

DR. PAUL DUDLEY WHITE
heart specialist:

"A man ought to have a doctor's prescription to be allowed to use a golf cart."

MAURICE LUCAS
Portland Trail Blazers forward, after a stern reprimand by coach Jack Ramsay for talking during stretching exercises:

"Jack LaLanne talks during *his* stretching exercises."

HENRY DAVID THOREAU
writer/philosopher:

"It's a great art to saunter."

HENRY DAVID THOREAU
writer/philosopher:

"If you are ready to leave father and mother, and brother and
sister, and wife and child and friends, and never see them again
—if you have paid your debts, and made your will, and settled
all your affairs, and are a free man, then you are ready for a
walk. . . ."

OSCAR WILDE
Irish poet/dramatist:

"The only possible form of exercise is to talk, not to walk."

BENJAMIN FRANKLIN
statesman/scientist/philosopher:

"Want of exercise occasions want of appetite, so that eating and
drinking afford but little pleasure."

HENRY FORD
auto manufacturer:

"Exercise is bunk. If you are healthy, you don't need it; if you
are sick, you shouldn't take it."

DENNY MCLAIN
Washington Senators pitcher:

"All that running and exercise can do for you is make you
healthy."

NEIL ARMSTRONG
former astronaut:

"I believe every human has a finite number of heartbeats. I
don't intend to waste any of mine running around doing exercises."

Experience

FRED SHERO
New York Rangers coach and general manager:

"Experience is the name we give our mistakes."

PAT CORRALES
Philadelphia Phillies manager:

"I was told by a very smart man a long time ago that talent always beats experience. Because by the time you get experience, the talent's gone."

DOUG RADER
former Houston Astros third baseman, on being passed over for the San Diego Padres managerial job because he lacked experience:

"The Pilgrims didn't have any experience when they landed here. Hell, if experience was that important, we'd never have anybody walking on the moon."

CASEY STENGEL
New York Yankees manager, when rookie outfielder Mickey Mantle seemed unimpressed with Stengel's knowledge of the game:

"He thinks that I was born at the age of 62 and started managing immediately."

Fame

SATCHEL PAIGE
former Negro league and major league pitcher, after being named to the baseball Hall of Fame's wing for old-time Negro players:

"The only change is that baseball has turned Paige from a second-class citizen to a second-class immortal."

JOE PATERNO
Penn State football coach:

"Publicity is like poison. It doesn't hurt unless you swallow it."

KEITH JACKSON
sportscaster, on awards:

"If you can't eat it, drink it, cash it or sleep with it, don't worry about it."

GERALD R. FORD
fortieth Vice President of the United States:

"If I had gone into professional football, the name Jerry Ford might be a household word today. But instead, I had to find a different way to make a living."

HENRY AARON
former Milwaukee/Atlanta Braves outfielder, upon his election to the Hall of Fame:

"I never wanted them to forget Babe Ruth. I just wanted them to remember Aaron."

JIM BOUTON
major league pitcher-turned-writer, shortly before his book *Ball Four* was released:

"I thought if I ever got to be famous or great I'd write a book about it. Unfortunately, I couldn't wait any longer."

CASEY STENGEL
New York Mets manager, asked about a pair of 20-year-olds on his roster:

"In 10 years, Ed Kranepool has a chance to be a star. In 10 years, Greg Goossen has a chance to be 30."

BILLY MARTIN
Detroit Tigers manager and possessor of the last bat used by Joe DiMaggio, stipulating a condition necessary for him to donate it to baseball's Hall of Fame:

"I want them to put a tag on the bat that I donated it. That's the only way I'll ever get in there."

REGGIE JACKSON
major league outfielder:

"I don't want to be a hero; I don't want to be a star. It just works out that way."

EDWARD KENNEDY
U.S. senator, accepting the Washington Touchdown Club's Gene Brito Award
on behalf of his son, Ted Jr.:

"For years I was introduced as the brother of the President of
the United States, and then I was introduced as the brother of
the Attorney General. And just when I begin to make it on my
own, I'm introduced as the father of the recipient."

Fans

RED SMITH
sportswriter:

"Rooting for the New York Yankees is like rooting for U.S. Steel."

JAMES MICHENER
writer, on the New York Yankees:

"They are the establishment, the Republican right wing. They represent everything that is conservative and objectionable in life. A really good year for me is when the Yankees are ahead by 11 games in mid-July, and then Boston comes on strong and beats them out. That is the way God intended that it should be."

ANDY STAURSKY
U.S. Steel publicist:

"On Monday mornings you can find a president of a Fortune 500 company, a regular salesman and a maintenance man in front of the U.S. Steel building talking football; and from the way they talk there would be no way in the world to distinguish their stations in life."

BILL VEECK
Chicago White Sox owner:

"I have discovered, in 20 years of moving around a ball park, that the knowledge of the game is usually in inverse proportion to the price of the seats."

ARTHUR DALEY
sportswriter:

"A baseball fan has the digestive apparatus of a billy goat. He can—and does—devour any set of statistics with insatiable appetite and then muzzle hungrily for more."

ART HILL
writer:

"I write from the viewpoint of the average fan, although, like any average fan, I think I know more about the game than the average fan."

MAYO SMITH
former Detroit Tigers manager:

"Detroit fans don't know anything about baseball. They couldn't tell the difference between baseball players and Japanese aviators."

BOB UECKER
sportscaster and former major league catcher, recalling his playing days in Philadelphia:

"Philly fans are so mean that one Easter Sunday, when the players staged an Easter-egg hunt for their kids, the fans booed the kids who didn't find any eggs."

JOE GARAGIOLA
sportscaster and former major league catcher:

"One thing you learn as a Cubs fan: When you bought your ticket, you could bank on seeing the bottom of the ninth."

FERGUSON JENKINS
major league pitcher, reflecting on his early years with the Chicago Cubs:

"I don't think those people at Wrigley Field ever saw but two players they liked—Billy Williams and Ernie Banks. Billy never said anything, and Ernie always said the right thing."

JEAN SHEPHERD
humorist:

"If I was going to storm a pillbox, going to sheer, utter, certain death, and the colonel said, 'Shepherd, pick six guys,' I'd pick six White Sox fans, because they have known death every day of their lives and it holds no terror for them."

JACK LAVELLE
New York Giants scout, after watching the Colts in Baltimore:

"I'm glad we don't have to play the Colt fans. They're tougher than the team."

ROCKY BRIDGES
minor league baseball manager:

"There are three things the average man thinks he can do better than anybody else: build a fire, run a hotel and manage a baseball team."

LOU HOLTZ
Arkansas football coach, after being pelted with oranges thrown by fans celebrating the Razorbacks' invitation to the Orange Bowl:

"I'm glad we're not going to the *Gator* Bowl."

BILL LEE
Montreal Expos pitcher, on why fans collect baseball cards:

"We live in a collecting society. Some people collect automobiles or guns, others just collect unemployment."

FRED DRYER
Los Angeles Rams linebacker, asked what Rams fans in Anaheim are like:

"Like Weber's Bread—all white, no substance."

TERRY BRADSHAW
Pittsburgh Steelers quarterback:

"When you're on the football field, they don't care about your beliefs; they don't care what kind of grades you made; they don't care who your dad is. All they want is for you to perform and perform well, period."

JOHN CHEEVER
writer:

"All literary men are Red Sox fans. To be a Yankee fan in literary society is to endanger your life."

JAMES MICHENER
writer:

"Bennett Cerf, my deceased publisher, always sensed that there was something about him I didn't like, something that kept us from being good friends. He finally asked me what it was, and I told him I could never be comfortable with anyone who was a Yankee fan, which he was. I told him I thought there was something fundamentally sick about being affiliated with the Yankees."

DAVID FREED
captain of America's 1961 Davis Cup team:

"I wasn't so upset the other day when a letter came addressed to 'David the Dope.' That's the privilege of all sports fans. But how did the post office know where to deliver the mail?"

(Duffy Daugherty, Michigan State football coach, after receiving a letter addressed to Duffy the Dope: "I didn't mind getting the card. The thing that bothered me was that the East Lansing post office knew exactly where to deliver it.")

AL FORMAN
major league umpire:

"I occasionally get birthday cards from fans. But it's often the same message: they hope it's my last."

JIM TUNNEY
NFL referee:

"My definition of a fan is the kind of guy who will scream at you from the 60th row of the bleachers because he thinks you missed a marginal holding call in the center of the interior line, and then after the game won't be able to find his car in the parking lot."

DANNY MURTAUGH
Pittsburgh Pirates manager:

"Why, certainly I'd like to have a fellow who hits a home run every time at bat, who strikes out every opposing batter when he's pitching, and who is always thinking about two innings ahead. The only trouble is to get him to put down his cup of beer, come down out of the stands and do those things."

MIKE MARSHALL
Minnesota Twins relief pitcher, on local fans who continually booed him:

"If they worked as hard at their jobs as I do at mine, this country wouldn't have the inflation problem it now has."

REGGIE JACKSON
New York Yankees outfielder, explaining why certain groups of Yankee Stadium fans didn't boo him when he returned to the lineup after a five-game suspension:

"All the fans in those sections are black, under 10 and don't read the papers."

TUBBY RAYMOND
Delaware football coach, asked why his team doesn't have a booster club:

"I don't want to organize my own lynching mob."

LILLIAN HELLMAN
playwright:

"Mr. Dashiell Hammett spoiled me of all sports. He was such a sports fan—a sports fiend, I should say—that he drove me crazy."

JOE MEDWICK
St. Louis Cardinals outfielder, after a barrage of fruit, garbage and cardboard boxes from fans in the left-field stands forced him to leave the seventh game of the 1934 World Series:

"I know why they threw it at me. What I can't figure out is why they brought it to the ball park in the first place."

STEVE DALEY
writer:

"There is no off-season in Chicago. It is only when the teams start playing that the fans lose interest."

THOMAS BOSWELL
sportswriter:

"All baseball fans can be divided into two groups: those who come to batting practice and the others. Only those in the first category have much chance of amounting to anything."

JOHN F. KENNEDY
thirty-fifth President of the United States, on whether America's national sport is baseball or football:

"The sad fact is that it looks more and more as if our national sport is not playing at all—but watching."

BUZZIE BAVASI
San Diego Padres president, on fan support for the rival Los Angeles Dodgers:

"Heck, in Los Angeles 20,000 people would show up at the park accidentally, just to see what the lights were about."

STEVE KREIDER
Cincinnati Bengals wide receiver, observing that 46,302 fans had turned out for a Bengals playoff game in 59-below-zero wind-chill conditions:

"It reflects the failure of our educational system."

WARREN G. HARDING
twenty-ninth President of the United States:

"I never saw a game without taking sides and never want to see one. There is the soul of the game."

GEORGE BERNARD SHAW
British playwright/novelist:

"What is both surprising and delightful is that [baseball] spectators are allowed, and even expected, to join in the vocal part of the game. I do not see why this feature should not be introduced into cricket. There is no reason why the field should not try to put the batsman off his stroke at the critical moment by neatly timed disparagements of his wife's fidelity and his mother's respectability."

Fear

WALT MICHAELS
New York Jets coach:

"Everyone has some fear. A man who has no fear belongs in a mental institution. Or on special teams."

VIKTOR KORCHNOI
chess grand master, asked if he feared playing Russian grand master Anatoly Karpov for the world championship in 1978:

"I fear nobody but the dentist."

JERRY LEVIAS
5'9" 177-pound Houston Oilers kick returner:

"When you're my size in the pros, fear is a sign that you're not stupid."

JOE TORRE
Atlanta Braves manager:

"You look at a guy who's being brave. He's afraid, or he wouldn't be brave. If he isn't afraid, he's stupid."

Fights

ROD GILBERT
New York Rangers right wing, asked if hockey fights are faked:

"If they were faked, you would see me in more of them."

CALVIN MURPHY
5'9" Houston Rockets guard:

"My theory on fighting is don't fight fair. Surprise them. Get them when they're coming out of church."

PHIL ESPOSITO
New York Rangers center:

"If they took away our sticks and gave us brooms, we'd still have fights."

JIM BOUTON
major league pitcher-turned-writer:

"Lots of people look up to Billy Martin. That's because he's just knocked them down."

BOB FERRY
Baltimore Bullets center, recalling a fight with Wilt Chamberlain:

"I threw a left hook, but I was backpedaling so fast it never got there."

CLARENCE CAMPBELL
NHL president:

"I've said it time and again, and I know that there are many students of human behavior who disagree with me. But, with my considerable experience, I feel that the safest and most satisfactory reaction to being fouled is by retaliating with a punch in the nose."

Fishing

HERBERT HOOVER
thirty-first President of the United States:

"Fishing is a . . . discipline in the equality of men—for all men are equal before fish."

HENRY VAN DYKE
writer:

"There is a peculiar pleasure in catching trout in a place where nobody thinks of looking for them, and at an hour when everybody believes they cannot be caught."

JOHN STEINBECK
writer:

"It has always been my private conviction that any man who pits his intelligence against a fish and loses has it coming."

HERBERT HOOVER
thirty-first President of the United States:

"There are only two occasions when Americans respect privacy, especially in Presidents. Those are prayer and fishing. So that some have taken to fishing."

STEPHEN LEACOCK
Canadian humorist:

"It is to be observed that 'angling' is the name given to fishing by people who can't fish."

SAMUEL JOHNSON
English critic:

"Angling—I can only compare to a stick and string, with a worm at one end and a fool at the other."

DON MARQUIS
humorist:

"Fishing is a delusion entirely surrounded by liars in old clothes."

IRVIN S. COBB
humorist:

"In literature, fishing is indeed an exhilarating sport; but, so far as my experience goes, it does not pan out when you carry the idea further."

MARK TWAIN
writer:

"There is no use in your walking five miles to fish when you can depend on being just as unsuccessful near home."

HERBERT HOOVER
thirty-first President of the United States:

"Fishing is the eternal fountain of youth. . . . There is said to be a tablet of 2000 B.C. which says: 'Gods do not subtract from the allotted span of men's lives the hours spent fishing.' "

DICK CAVETT
television commentator, telling of a fisherman on the polluted Hudson River who hooked an undersized fish:

"The fish begged the man not to throw him back."

BOB DEVANEY
Nebraska athletic director, claiming Husker football coach Tom Osborne was such a great fisherman that a game warden once accompanied him to learn his technique:

"Tom took the game warden out in the middle of the lake, lit a stick of dynamite, threw it in the water and fish were flying everywhere. After a few minutes, he handed the game warden a stick of dynamite and said, 'Are you going to fish or are you just going to sit there?' "

Football

JACK KEMP
New York congressman and former NFL quarterback:

"Pro football gave me a good sense of perspective to enter politics. I'd already been booed, cheered, cut, sold, traded and hung in effigy."

KENNETH SIMS
New England Patriots defensive lineman:

"Football is football. The best high school players usually make the best college players, and the best college players usually make the best pro players. It's just that the cream gets a little thinner and thinner as you go along, because the weave of the strainer gets tighter and tighter."

VINCE LOMBARDI
Green Bay Packers coach:

"This is a game for madmen."

NORM VAN BROCKLIN
former NFL player and coach:

"There's no tougher way to make easy money than pro football."

CHARLES HORTON COOLEY
sociologist:

"There is a function of a quasi-religious nature performed by a few experts but followed in spirit by the whole university world, serving indeed as a symbol to arouse in the students and in the alumni certain congregate and hieratic emotions. I refer, of course, to football."

VINCE LOMBARDI
Green Bay Packers coach:

"Football is blocking and tackling. Everything else is mythology."

LOU HOLTZ
Arkansas football coach, on one of football's most revered statistics:

"The only important thing about the time of possession is who gets to keep the ball after the game is over."

CALVIN COOLIDGE
thirtieth President of the United States, upon being introduced to "George Halas and Red Grange of the Chicago Bears":

"How are you, young gentlemen? I have always admired animal acts."

DUANE THOMAS
NFL running back, on the Super Bowl:

"If it's the ultimate, how come they're playing it again next year?"

HENRY MACCRACKEN
New York University chancellor, on the state of college football in the early twentieth century:

"The game has no social significance, except to give ruffians on our campuses an opportunity to express themselves."

ELBERT HUBBARD
writer:

"Football—a sport that bears the same relation to education that bullfighting does to agriculture."

TAD JONES
Yale football coach:

"Gentlemen, you are about to play a game against Harvard. Nothing you do in life will ever again be so important as what you do on that field today."

FRANZ LIDZ
sportswriter:

"One of my uncles was a classic paranoid who couldn't sit through a football game. He thought the guys in the huddle were talking about him."

GEORGE SAUER, JR.
New York Jets receiver:

"As a wide receiver I'm always running for my life, learning that to be an outsider is the ultimate achievement."

SALLY QUINN
writer:

"The football season is like pain. You forget how terrible it is until it seizes you again."

RONALD REAGAN
governor of California:

"It's a game in which you can feel a clean hatred for your opponent."

BOB ZUPPKE
Illinois football coach:

"Dancing is a contact sport. Football is a hitting sport."
   (Duffy Daugherty, Michigan State football coach: "Football is not a contact sport. It's a collision sport. Dancing is a good example of a contact sport.")

SHAILER MATHEWS
Chicago Divinity School dean, on football of the late nineteenth century:

"Football today is a social obsession. Football is a boy-killing, education-prostituting, gladiatorial sport. It teaches virility and courage, but so does war. I do not know what should take its place, but the new game should not require the services of a physician, the maintenance of a hospital, and the celebration of funerals."

LYNDON B. JOHNSON
thirty-sixth President of the United States:

"To see some of our best-educated boys spending the afternoon knocking each other down, while thousands cheer them on, hardly gives a picture of a peace-loving nation."

GEORGE F. WILL
writer, defining the sport:

"It is committee meetings, called huddles, separated by outbursts of violence."

CARL DEPASQUA
Pitt football coach:

"Football is not a democracy. There's nothing to debate. The players can debate in political science class."

FRANK GIFFORD
New York Giants halfback-turned-sportscaster:

"Pro football is like nuclear warfare. There are no winners, only survivors."

DARRELL ROYAL
Texas football coach:

"Football doesn't build character. It eliminates the weak ones."

REV. PAUL L. O'CONNOR
Xavier (Ohio) University president:

"If you finish above .500, the NCAA will investigate you. If you finish below .500, the alumni will investigate you."

TERRY BRADSHAW
Pittsburgh Steelers quarterback:

"This isn't nuclear physics, it's a game. How smart do you really have to be?"

JERRY WELCH
Arkansas offensive guard:

"When the defense does its job, it's in there just three plays, but when we do our job right, we're out there all day."

WALTER CAMP
Yale football coach:

"When it comes to the football field, mind will always win over muscle and brute force."

AL DENSON
Denver Broncos wide receiver, on what it's like to catch a pass and be tackled simultaneously:

"It's like walking out of a store with a bag of groceries and getting hit by a car. Sometimes you don't care what happens to the bag."

WALTER CAMP
Yale football coach, on football in the late nineteenth century:

"We have lost the Homeric thrill of human action, the zest of out-of-doors, the contest of speed, of strength, of human intelligence, of courage. Unless steps are taken to reform the sport, we shall discover that our precious football is being relegated to the ash heap of history. Brutality has no place in this sport. This is a game that must train its followers, its players and its spectators in the qualities of successful character. They are: knowledge, skill, strength, speed, obedience, initiative, aggressiveness, courage, honor, and morale."

JOHN BRIDGERS
Baylor football coach:

"We're a Baptist school, and in football we strive for the same spirit as the three Baptists who were shipwrecked on a deserted island and immediately set a Sunday School attendance goal of four."

JONES RAMSEY
Texas University publicist:

"There are only two sports at Texas—football and spring football."

JOHN HEISMAN
college football coach/Shakespearean actor, displaying a football to his squad and explaining what it was, a ritual he performed on the first day of practice each season:

"A prolate spheroid—that is, an elongated sphere—in which the outer leathern casing is drawn tightly over a somewhat smaller rubber tubing. [Dramatic pause] Better to have died as a small boy than to fumble this."

ANONYMOUS
from the *London Economist,* on pro football's effect on the college game:

"Amateur standing in American football is like virginity—highly prized but difficult to ascertain."

JIM HENSON
Muppets creator, on why Miss Piggy refused to join him at University of Maryland homecoming festivities:

"She heard they were kicking around a pigskin and that all those people were eating hot dogs. She thought the whole thing was sort of barbaric."

HERMAN HICKMAN
Yale football coach and reputed inventor of "special teams":

"In modern football you can't win with iron men anymore. I have three special teams—one for offense, one for defense, and one to hit the books."

FIELDING YOST
Michigan football coach:

"Football games aren't won—they're lost."

BALL CARRIERS AND RUSHING

JOHN MCKAY
University of Southern California football coach, to those who criticized him for letting running back O. J. Simpson carry the ball too much:

"Why not? It isn't very heavy. And besides, he doesn't belong to any union."

BUM PHILLIPS
New Orleans Saints coach, comparing Earl Campbell and George Rogers:

"Rogers *sees* daylight. Campbell *makes* daylight."

BOB NEWHART
comedian, on his days as a high school running back:

"Every time I went into the line on a fake I shouted, 'I don't have it!' "

JOHN MCKAY
University of Southern California football coach:

"A runner must understand that there's one bad thing about carrying that football—it attracts a crowd."

DOUG SHIVELY
Arizona Wranglers coach, on the New Jersey Generals' use of running back Herschel Walker as a blocker:

"It's like asking Liberace to carry the piano."

BOB ZUPPKE
Illinois football coach, upon hearing that Michigan coach Fielding Yost had commented that all Red Grange could do was run:

"All Galli-Curci can do is sing."

DEFENSE

CHUCK NOLL
Pittsburgh Steelers coach:

"Before you can win a game, you have to not lose it."

BOWDEN WYATT
Tennessee football coach, defining defensive "pursuit":

"Taking the shortest distance to the ball carrier and arriving in bad humor."

(Later attributed to Lou Holtz, Arkansas football coach Fred Shero, professional hockey coach, is credited with: "Take the shortest route to the puck carrier—and arrive in ill humor.")

EDDIE LEWIS
San Francisco 49ers cornerback:

"Playing cornerback is like being on an island; people can see you but they can't help you."

LEROY IRVIN
Kansas defensive back, on why he talks to opposing receivers:

"I just want 'em to know who's robbin' the train."

DAVE RIMINGTON
Nebraska offensive lineman, after lifting a piano into place at a team banquet so teammate Anthony Steels could sing and play:

"The coaches speak of skilled and nonskilled positions. Now I know the difference. Moving the piano is nonskill. Playing the piano is skill."

JIM MARSHALL
Minnesota Vikings defensive end, after scooping up a San Francisco fumble and running 66 yards into the wrong end zone:

"I saw my teammates running down the sidelines. I thought they were cheering for me."

JOHN BREEN
Houston Oilers executive, on why the Oilers' offense was ineffective:

"We were tipping off our plays. Whenever we broke from the huddle, three backs were laughing and one was pale as a ghost."

KICKERS

LOU GROZA
NFL placekicker:

"Old placekickers never die, they just go on missing the point."

LARRY LACEWELL
Arkansas State football coach, on placekicker Jim Hatfield:

"This is the first time I've had a kicker who could play with pain. Most of them play with passports."

BUM PHILLIPS
Houston Oilers coach, after Toni Fritsch kicked a field goal to give the Oilers an overtime win over the New York Jets:

"Every time I look up and see that kid on the field, I thank God for the immigration laws."

DON ADAMS
comedian:

"A good quarterback and a good receiver should go hand in hand—but not off the field."

JOHN HADL
San Diego Chargers quarterback, asked if the crowd's boos bothered him:

"No, I'm strictly a beer-drinker."

JOHN BRODIE
San Francisco 49ers veteran, asked why a million-dollar quarterback has to hold the ball for field goals and extra points:

"Well, if I didn't it would fall over."

LINEMEN

ADAM WALSH
Notre Dame lineman during the era of the Four Horsemen backfield:

"We are just the seven mules. We do all the work so that these four fellows can gallop into fame."

KNUTE ROCKNE
Notre Dame football coach:

"The result of any vote on a football team will always be seven to four."

RUSS FRANCIS
New England Patriots tight end, on defensive linemen:

"If their IQs were five points lower, they would be geraniums."

MERLIN OLSEN
Los Angeles Rams offensive lineman:

"Linemen are motivated by a more complicated, self-determining series of factors than the simple fear of humiliation in the public gaze which is the emotion that galvanizes the backs and receivers."

JOHN GORDY
Detroit Lions guard, on why the terms *offensive* and *defensive* as applied to linemen are inaccurate:

"I'm called an offensive lineman because our team's on offense, but what I'm trying to do is keep an aggressor from knocking me down and getting at my home and family. I'm defending."

JIM MURRAY
sportswriter:

"The interior line must be where guys on the lam from the police hide out. They're as anonymous as telephone operators."

LARRY CSONKA
New York Giants running back, on his team's selection of 6'5" 285-pound offensive tackle Gordon King in the college draft:

"It's good to have a lineman you can look straight in the belly button."

KNUTE ROCKNE
Notre Dame football coach:

"The only qualifications to be a lineman are to be big and dumb.
To be a back you only have to be dumb."

BILLY SIMS
Oklahoma running back, asked near the end of his senior year if his 247-yard game against Nebraska was the best of his college career:

"I don't know. I've got one game left."

JOHNNY LUJACK
Notre Dame quarterback, asked by coach Frank Leahy why he had thrown three interceptions to Army's Arnold Tucker:

"Coach, he was the only man open."

JACK KEMP
former Buffalo Bills quarterback, explaining how he won reelection to Congress in 1972:

"I told the people that if they didn't reelect me I'd come back as a quarterback of the Bills."

QUARTERBACKS AND QUARTERBACKING

FRANK GIFFORD
sportscaster on quarterbacks:

"They're the most poorly conditioned athletes we have. They're also old and crotchety."

FRAN TARKENTON
New York Giants quarterback:

"A quarterback is paid better, cheered more, often booed more. But a quarterback is not loved."

ANONYMOUS:

"Old quarterbacks never die, they just drop back and pass away."

SONNY JURGENSEN
Washington Redskins quarterback:

"It's like holding group therapy for 50,000 people a week."

JIM ZORN
Seattle Seahawks quarterback, on the art of scrambling in the NFL:

"You have to know when and how to go down. The key is to have a fervent desire to be in on the next play."

FRAN TARKENTON
Minnesota Vikings quarterback, on the need for protective blocking:

"I've been playing this game for 18 years, and I haven't yet figured a way to get into the end zone when you're on your rear end."

RED SANDERS
college football coach:

"He who lives by the pass, dies by the pass."

WOODY HAYES
Ohio State football coach:

"He who lives by the pass, dies by the run."

DOUG WILLIAMS
Tampa Bay Buccaneers quarterback, asked how he felt about coach John McKay's decision to bench him in the fourth quarter after he had thrown four interceptions against the Chicago Bears:

"I thought it was a hell of a move."

JACK THOMPSON
Washington State quarterback:

"It's amazing what the human body can do when chased by a bigger human body."

DUFFY DAUGHERTY
Michigan State football coach:

"Only three things can happen when you put a ball up in the air—and two of them are bad."

TERRY HANRATTY
former Notre Dame quarterback, asked whether his college uniform number had been retired:

"If they retired the numbers of all the greats at Notre Dame, there wouldn't be any numbers left."

SAMMY BAUGH
Washington Redskins quarterback, asked if the coming season would be his last:

"I don't know. I haven't tried it. Maybe last year was."

Gambling

HEYWOOD HALE BROUN
sportswriter/broadcaster:

"The urge to gamble is so universal and its practice so pleasurable that I assume it must be evil."

DAMON RUNYON
sportswriter:

"It may be that the race is not always to the swift nor the battle to the strong—but that is the way to bet."

PAUL LYNDE
comedian, on how to cure a compulsive gambler:

"Give him the Atlanta Falcons and four points."

DAMON RUNYON
sportswriter:

"In all human affairs, the odds are always 6 to 5 against."

PETE AXTHELM
sportswriter:

"I can't stand to look at a team that hasn't beaten the spread and thinks it's won."

LARRY GUEST
sportswriter:

"The way inflation is going, the old bet 'dollar to a doughnut' will soon be an even-money wager."

EARL WILSON
entertainment writer:

"No horse can go as fast as the money you put on it."

KIN HUBBARD
humorist:

"The more horse sense a fellow has the less he bets on 'em."

BILL LUNDERMAN
"All-Around Cowboy" titleholder in 1954:

"Rodeoing is about the only sport you can't fix. You'd have to talk to the bulls and horses, and they wouldn't understand you."

OSCAR WILDE
Irish poet/dramatist; defining horse sense:

"What keeps horses from betting on what people will do?"

WILL ROGERS
humorist:

"You know horses are smarter than people. You never heard of a horse going broke betting on people."

DON BRUMFIELD
jockey, asked by a fan at the track to pick a winner:

"If I knew what horse would win I wouldn't be riding. I'd be betting."

ARA PARSEGHIAN
former Notre Dame football coach, recalling a game against the University of Southern California after which a fan accosted him with a penknife:

"The game was at South Bend, but I wasn't sure if the guy was a Southern Cal fan and mad because we won, or a Notre Dame fan and mad because we didn't cover the betting spread."

WALTER HAGEN
professional golfer, after betting $10 he could sink his tee shot on a short hole and then doing it:

"The idea, when betting even money on a 100,000-to-1 shot, is to recognize the one time when it comes along. It is done by clean living."

LEE CORSO
Indiana football coach:

"There's a direct correlation between the hate mail you receive and the guy on the corner's ability to win or lose money."

CLETE BOYER
Hawaii Islander third baseman, on a $1,000 fine levied against him for gambling:

"I'd go double or nothing with Bowie Kuhn, but I don't think he'd go for that."

JOE SCHMIDT
Detroit Lions coach, on hearing that his quarterback, Bill Munson, might be subpoenaed to testify in a gambling inquiry:

"I know Munson hasn't done anything wrong. I'd bet my house on it."

MAXIE ROSENBLOOM
former light-heavyweight champion:

"Once some gamblers made me a very attractive offer to take a dive in the second round, but I turned them down. I couldn't go the distance."

ALEX KARRAS
Detroit Lions defensive lineman once suspended for betting on games, asked by an official to call a coin flip at midfield before a game:

"I can't do that, sir. I'm not allowed to gamble."

DAMON RUNYON
sportswriter:

"One of these days in your travels, a guy is going to come to you and show you a nice, brand-new deck of cards on which the seal is not yet broken, and this guy is going to offer to bet you that he can make the jack of spades jump out of the deck and squirt cider in your ear. But, son, do not bet this man, for as sure as you stand there, you are going to wind up with an earful of cider."

Golf

LEE TREVINO
professional golfer, on the four-course setup at the Bob Hope tournament in Palm Springs:

"The only problem is that it's hell to find your way home every night."

CHARLIE BOSWELL
blind golfer, after a player lashed at the ball during a benefit tournament:

"Worst swing I ever heard."

GERRY CHEEVERS
NHL goalie, asked how he was faring in a golf tournament:

"I'm one under. One under a tree, one under a rock, one under a bush . . ."

JACK BURKE
professional golfer, upon learning Arnold Palmer had brought eight putters to a tournament:

"That's a bag full of indecision."

SAM SNEAD
professional golfer:

"The only reason I played golf was so I could afford to go fishing and hunting."

GRANTLAND RICE
sportswriter:

"Eighteen holes of match or medal play will teach you more about your foe than will 18 years of dealing with him across a desk."

BERNARD DARWIN
English golfer and writer:

"Golf is not a funeral, though both can be very sad affairs."

BERTIE CHARLES FORBES
magazine editor:

"Golf is an ideal diversion, but a ruinous disease."

WESTBROOK PEGLER
sportswriter:

"Golf was, I should say offhand, the most useless outdoor game ever devised to waste the time and try the spirit of man."

IRVIN S. COBB
humorist:

"Golf . . . a young man's vice and an old man's penance."

GARY PLAYER
professional golfer:

"When you play for fun, it's fun. But when you play golf for a living, it's a game of sorrows. You're never happy."

TOMMY AARON
professional golfer:

"Golf is mostly a game of failures."

BOB HOPE
comedian:

"If you watch a game, it's fun. If you play it, it's recreation. If you work at it, it's golf."

BURT SHOTTEN
major league baseball manager:

"Any game where a man 60 can beat a man 30 ain't no game."

MARK TWAIN
writer:

"Golf is good walk spoiled."

WOODROW WILSON
twenty-eighth President of the United States, defining the sport:

"A game in which one endeavors to control a ball with implements ill adapted for the purposes."

ARNOLD DALY
actor:

"Golf is like a love affair: If you don't take it seriously, it's no fun; if you do take it seriously, it breaks your heart."

BRUCE CRAMPTON
professional golfer, on tournament play:

"It's a compromise between what your ego wants you to do, what experience tells you to do, and what your nerves let you do."

GEORGE PLIMPTON
writer:

"Golf cannot be played in anger, or in any mood of emotional excess. Half the golf balls struck by amateurs are hit if not in rage surely in bewilderment, or gloom, or cynicism, or even hysterically—all of those emotional excesses which must be contained by the professional. Which is why, because emotional balance is one of the essential ingredients of golf, professionals invariably trudge phlegmatically around the course—whatever emotions are seething within—with the grim yet placid and bored look of cowpokes, slack-bodied in their saddles, who have been tending the same herd for two months."

SAM SNEAD
professional golfer:

"If a lot of people gripped a knife and fork like they do a golf club, they'd starve to death."

JACK BENNY
comedian:

"Give me golf clubs, fresh air and a beautiful partner, and you can keep my golf clubs and the fresh air."

BOB HOPE
comedian, on the golf game of entertainer Sammy Davis, Jr.:

"He hits the ball 130 yards and his jewelry goes 150."

RICHARD M. NIXON
thirty-seventh President of the United States, on allegations that G. Harold Carswell, Supreme Court nominee, once belonged to a restricted golf club:

"I can only say that with regard to the restricted golf club that if everybody in Washington in government service who belongs or has belonged to a restricted golf club was to leave government service, this city would have the highest rate of unemployment of any city in the country."

CHI CHI RODRIGUEZ
professional golfer, on Jack Nicklaus' infrequent tournament appearances:

"He's the only golfer in history who has become a living legend in his spare time."

ALEX KARRAS
Detroit Lions defensive lineman, to a startled employee of the Red Run Golf Club in Royal Oak, Michigan, after hitting a golf ball off the first tee through a large plate glass window in the clubhouse:

"Hey, is this room out of bounds?"

HARRY TOSCANO
professional golfer:

"I'm hitting the woods just great, but I'm having a terrible time getting out of them."

PAUL HARVEY
news commentator, after Jack Nicklaus shot an 83 in the first round of the 1981 British Open:

"All my life I wanted to play golf like Jack Nicklaus, and now I do."

JIM COLBERT
professional golfer, refusing to get overly optimistic after posting an early lead in a tournament:

"The slums of Chicago are full of first-round leaders."

DAVID BRENNER
comedian:

"I don't like to watch golf on television. I can't stand whispering."

BOB HOPE
comedian:

"I'd give up golf if I didn't have so many sweaters."

ALEX KARRAS
Detroit Lions defensive lineman:

"My best score ever is 103, but I've only been playing 15 years."

DEREK HARDY
teaching pro, on why he charges $140 for a series of 13 lessons yet demands $1,000 for a single session:

"If you expect a miracle, you should expect to pay for one."

LEE TREVINO
professional golfer:

"There are two things not long for this world—dogs that chase cars and pro golfers who chip for pars."

LEE TREVINO
professional golfer, praising Billy Casper for his performance as captain of the victorious 1979 Ryder Cup team:

"He fouled up once. He never got the bar set up in the players' lounge."

ABE LEMONS
Texas basketball coach, explaining how he came within two strokes of winning an automobile in a golf tournament:

"It was a hole-in-one contest and I had a three."

BOB HOPE
comedian, after a round of golf with labor leader George Meany:

"He plays just like a union man. He negotiates the final score."

WALTER HAGEN
professional golfer:

"Every golfer can expect to have four bad shots a round. When you do, just put them out of your mind."
   (Jim Murray, sports columnist: "This, of course, is hard to do when you're not even off the first tee after you've had them.")

SAM SNEAD
professional golfer:

"Forget your opponents; always play against par."

TOMMY BOLT
professional golfer:

"If you are going to throw a club, it is important to throw it ahead of you, down the fairway, so you don't waste energy going back to pick it up."

LEE TREVINO
professional golfer:

"You can talk to a fade, but a hook won't listen."

SAMUEL JOHNSON
English critic:

"It is unjust to claim the privileges of age and retain the playthings of childhood."

G. K. CHESTERTON
English writer:

"Golf is an expensive way of playing marbles."

KEITH JACKSON
sportscaster:

"Never have so many spent so much to sit in relative comfort to brag about their failures."

WILL ROGERS
humorist:

"Rail-splitting produced an immortal president in Abraham Lincoln; but golf, with 29,000 courses, hasn't produced even a good A-Number-1 congressman."

GRANTLAND RICE
sportswriter:

It matters not the sacrifice
Which makes the duffer's wife so sore
I am the captive of my slice
I am the servant of my score.

JOE E. LOUIS
comedian:

"I play in the low 80s. If it's any hotter than that, I won't play."

PAUL GALLICO
sportswriter:

"If there is any larceny in a man, golf will bring it out."

WILLIE NELSON
country singer, asked what par is on a golf course he purchased near Austin, Texas:

"Anything I want it to be. For instance, this hole right here is a par 47—and yesterday I birdied the sucker."

GEORGE ARCHER
professional golfer:

"If it wasn't for golf, I'd probably be a caddie today."

JACK NICKLAUS
professional golfer, asked why he tees up his ball so high:

"Through years of experience I have found that air offers less resistance than dirt."

JOHN MCKAY
Tampa Bay Buccaneers coach, explaining why he doesn't want to develop a slow backswing to improve his golf:

"If I had one, it would take me 4 hours to play. I can play in 2 hours 15 minutes with the one I have now."

JIM DENT
professional golfer known for his long tee shots:

"I can airmail the golf ball, but sometimes I don't put the right address on it."

LEE TREVINO
professional golfer, responding to a woman who saw him washing windows at his Dallas home and inquired as to how much he charged for his services:

"Lady, the woman in this house lets me sleep with her."

ROBERT LYND
sociologist/professor:

"It is almost impossible to remember how tragic a place the world is when one is playing golf."

132

Good Losers

RED BLAIK
Army football coach:

"There was never a champion who to himself was a good loser. There's a vast difference between a good sport and a good loser."

LEO DUROCHER
major league manager:

"Show me a good loser in professional sports, and I'll show you an idiot. Show me a sportsman, and I'll show you a player I'm looking to trade."

KNUTE ROCKNE
Notre Dame football coach:

"Show me a good and gracious loser and I'll show you a failure."

O. J. SIMPSON
San Francisco 49ers running back:

"Show me a guy who is a gracious loser and I'll show you a perennial loser."

GENE FULLMER
middleweight boxing champion:

"If there's a good loser in boxing, I'd like to fight him every week."

BILLY MARTIN
Oakland A's manager:

"If there is such a thing as a good loser, then the game is crooked."

BOB ZUPPKE
Illinois football coach:

"All quitters are good losers."
   (Thought by some to have been the basis for "Quitters never win, and winners never quit.")

BLAINE NYE
Dallas Cowboys lineman:

"It's not whether you win or lose, but who gets the blame."

Heroes

MIKE ERUZIONE
captain of the gold-medal–winning 1980 U.S. Olympic hockey team:

"Hero? Vietnam vets are heroes. The guys who tried to rescue our hostages in Iran are heroes. I'm just a hockey player."

JAMES GARNER
actor, after attending a sports celebrity awards dinner:

"I felt like my bubble-gum card collection had come to life."

BILL RUSSELL
former Boston Celtics center:

"I've never seen an athlete, including myself, who I think should be lionized. There are very few athletes I know whom I would want my kids to be like. The only kids I try to set an example for are mine."

STEVEN HUNT
New York Cosmos soccer player:

"People assume that my greatest thrill last year was winning the championship. They're wrong. It was meeting Mick Jagger."

BOB ZUPPKE
Illinois football coach:

"The hero of a thousand plays becomes a bum after one error."

JIM MURRAY
sportswriter:

"The public never forgives a guy who dents an idol, profanes an icon or shows up Santa Claus. You can kill all the buffalo, wipe out the cavalry, rob all the banks, sell the State house, run rum or join the Mafia—but don't mess around with America's sports idolatry.

"They don't forgive the guy who floored Dempsey, beat Willie Pep, ambushed Billy the Kid, hit more homers than Babe Ruth, shot more birdies than Hogan or overtook Arnold Palmer."

Hockey

FRANK DEFORD
sportswriter:

"Hockey's the only place where a guy can go nowadays and watch two white guys fight."

FRED SHERO
professional hockey coach:

"If they want pretty skating, let 'em go to the Ice Capades."

GENE SHUE
Baltimore Bullets coach, on hockey radio broadcasts:

"It's like listening to a description of one continuous mistake."

JIMMY CANNON
sportswriter, defining a puck:

"A hard rubber disk that hockey players strike when they can't hit one another."

CONN SMYTHE
Toronto Maple Leafs owner:

"If you can't beat 'em in the alley, you can't beat 'em on the ice."

JACK KENT COOKE
Los Angeles Kings owner, on his team's feeble drawing power:

"There are 800,000 Canadians living in the L.A. area, and I've just discovered why they left Canada. They hate hockey."

EMORY JONES
St. Louis Arena general manager:

"Hockey players are like mules. They have no fear of punishment and no hope of reward."

CLIVE CHARLES
Portland Timbers hockey player, asked who would be the one person in the world he would most like to meet:

"The guy who stole my suede coat."

135

Horse Racing and Jockeys

ROGER KAHN
writer:

"Horse racing is animated roulette."

FRANK "PANCHO" MARTIN
horse trainer, on whether he develops feelings for his horses:

"Sentiment is for your family. Horses is a business, not sentiment."

DUFFY DAUGHERTY
Michigan State football coach, describing California's Santa Anita Park:

"The only place where windows clean people."
   (Danny Thomas, comedian: "A racetrack is a place where windows clean people.")

JACK O'HARA
New York racetrack clerk of scales:

"The race rider has the paradox of being one of the few men able to afford his own gourmet cook—and the only one who can't afford to eat the cooking."

MELVIN "SUNSHINE" CALVERT
horse trainer:

"To me a horse is like a bar of soap. Every time you wash your hands, you take a little of the bar away."

LENNY GOODMAN
jockey agent:

"I try to keep myself in the best of company and my horses in the worst of company."

WILL ROGERS
humorist:

"Lincoln went down in history as 'Honest Abe,' but he never was a jockey. If he had been a jockey, he might have gone down as just 'Abe.' "

"SUNNY JIM" FITZSIMMONS
trainer, at age 83:

"I'll be around as long as the horses think I'm smarter than they are."

STEVE CAUTHEN
jockey:

"The horse weighs one thousand pounds and I weigh ninety-five. I guess I'd better get him to cooperate."

DIANE CRUMP
jockey:

"A horse doesn't know whether the rider on his back wears a dress or pants away from the track."

SAMMY RENICK
jockey, on female riders:

"The only one I ever heard of to make a historical contribution was Lady Godiva."

SONNEY WERKMAN
jockey:

"Two things there ain't in this world—lady hookers and gentleman jockeys."

RED SMITH
sportswriter:

"Horse players love to suffer. They are never truly happy unless they are miserable—freezing or sweltering or drenched by rain, shiny in the seat and tissue-thin in the sole, elbowed and trampled and bruised in cramped space where the air they breathe has already been breathed several times, unable to find a slat to sit on or a winner to back, stone broke and sinking hopelessly deeper into debt."

JIM MURRAY
sportswriter:

"A racetrack crowd comprises the greatest floating fund of misinformation this side of the pages of *Pravda,* the last virgin stand of optimism in our century."

MARY BACON
jockey, recalling a 1969 race that was run six days before she became a mother:

"My mount that day was a mare in foal. I couldn't help but think about those fans betting on a pregnant horse ridden by a pregnant jockey. The four of us finished last."

SI BURICK
sportswriter, on thoroughbred Secretariat:

"He's everything I'm not. He's young; he's beautiful; he has lots of hair; he's fast; he's durable; he has a large bank account; and his entire sex life is before him."

JOHN GALBREATH
Pittsburgh Pirates president and owner of two Kentucky Derby winners, on the advantages of dealing with Derby winners:

"You don't have to feed him any more the day after the race than you fed him the day before the race, and you don't have to sign him up for next year."

HERB STEVENS
trainer, on assertions that Rockhill Native was too small a horse to win the Kentucky Derby:

"If size meant anything, a cow could beat a rabbit."

Hunting

GRANTLAND RICE
sportswriter, claiming hunting was his favorite outdoor activity besides golf:

"This, despite the fact that every place I hunted I established as a sanctuary. There always seemed to be more birds there when I left than when I came."

GEORGE BERNARD SHAW
British playwright/novelist:

"When a man wants to murder a tiger he calls it sport, when a tiger wants to murder him he calls it ferocity."

JOSEPH WOOD KRUTCH
writer:

"When a man wantonly destroys one of the works of man we call him a vandal. When he wantonly destroys one of the works of God we call him a sportsman."

STEPHEN LEACOCK
Canadian humorist:

"A sportsman is a man who, every now and then, simply has to get out and kill something."

P. G. WODEHOUSE
English writer:

"The fascination of shooting as a sport depends almost wholly on whether you are at the right or wrong end of the gun."

OSCAR WILDE
Irish poet/dramatist:

"The English country gentleman galloping after a fox—the unspeakable in full pursuit of the uneatable."

DR. FELIX B. GEAR
reverend:

"I have hunted deer on occasion, but they were not aware of it."

GRANTLAND RICE
sportswriter, in response to hunting partners who called him a "sissy" when he failed to pull the trigger on a whitetail deer:

"It's not that, exactly. It's just that I never shoot a deer until he pulls a knife on me first."

Improvident Pronouncements

ANONYMOUS CRITIC
The New York Times, on the first live telecast of a sporting event—a 1939 baseball game between Princeton and Columbia:

"It is difficult to see how this sort of thing can catch the public fancy."

JIMMY POWERS
New York *Daily News* sports editor, when Jackie Robinson became the first black player to sign a modern professional baseball contract:

"Robinson will not make the grade in the major leagues. He is a thousand-to-one shot at best. The Negro players simply don't have the brains or the skills."

TRIS SPEAKER
Cleveland Indians manager, on Babe Ruth, early in the slugger's career:

"Ruth made a grave mistake when he gave up pitching. Working once a week, he might have lasted a long time and become a great star."

POP WARNER
College football coach from 1895 through 1938, on Clark Shaughnessy's innovative T formation:

"If Stanford wins a single game with that crazy formation, you can throw all the football I ever knew into the Pacific Ocean."

Stanford had won only one game the previous season, but in 1940 with the "T," the Indians won the Pacific Coast Conference and then beat Nebraska in the 1941 Rose Bowl.

Injuries

VINCE LOMBARDI
Green Bay Packers coach:

"No one is ever hurt. Hurt is in the mind."
  (Also attributed to Lombardi's father)

BILL VEECK
Chicago White Sox owner, reflecting
on the chronic pain eminating from
what remains of his nearly fully
amputated left leg:

"Suffering is overrated. It
doesn't teach you anything."

BOB KEARNEY
Miami Dolphins publicist, on the
team's coach:

"Don Shula has a high
threshold of pain for someone
else's pain."

GARRY UNGER
Atlanta Flames hockey player:

"It's difficult to play hurt—in fact, it's difficult to play when
you're healthy."

BOBBY HULL
Winnipeg Jets hockey player, on playing with injuries:

"There is no better tonic for a hockey player than scoring a
goal."

GORDIE HOWE
Hall of Fame hockey player, asked if he had ever broken his nose during play:

"No, but 11 other guys did."

SANDY KOUFAX
Los Angeles Dodgers pitcher, upon sustaining an injury that sidelined him
during one of his best seasons:

"I feel like Job. I can't get mad at anybody except the Lord, and
if I do that I'm afraid things will get worse."

DR. ROBERT RAY
orthopedic surgeon:

"If God had intended man to engage in strenuous sports, He
would have given us better knees."

JOHN O'LEARY
Montreal Alouettes running back, upon retiring due to a neck injury:

"The doctors told me there are two things I can't do—play
football or dive into empty swimming pools."

RON HUNT
Montreal Expos infielder and perennial season leader for times hit by the pitch:

"Some people give their bodies to science; I gave mine to baseball."

TOM LANDRY
Dallas Cowboys coach, after quarterback Roger Staubach suffered a slight concussion in an exhibition game:

"I was delighted it was his head and not his knee."

BILL VEECK
Chicago White Sox owner and possessor of a wooden leg, after injuring his *good* leg:

"It's a pity it couldn't have been the other leg. I could have called a carpenter."

BILL MUNCEY
Thunderboat racer, after surviving a serious crash:

"Anything other than death is a minor injury."

Intelligence

DUANE THOMAS,
Dallas Cowboys running back, asked if he possessed an IQ:

"Sure I've got one. It's a perfect 20-20."

DIZZY DEAN
major league pitcher, upon his induction into baseball's Hall of Fame:

"The Good Lord was good to me. He gave me a strong body, a good right arm and a weak mind."

FRANK LAYDEN
Utah Jazz general manager, recalling an Atlanta player from his days as the Hawks' assistant coach:

"We got a pretty good reading on this fellow when we glimpsed the information sheet he filled out for our public relations department. On the line where 'church preference' was requested, the guy wrote 'red brick.' "

FRED TAYLOR
Ohio State basketball coach, on rebellious players of the early seventies whose actions led to a number of coaching resignations:

"You could put the brains of three of those guys in a hummingbird and it would still fly backwards."

TALLULAH BANKHEAD
actress:

"There have been only two geniuses in the world—Willie Mays and Willie Shakespeare."

Jogging

ABE LEMONS
Texas basketball coach, on why he doesn't jog:

"If I die, I want to be sick."

MILTON BERLE
comedian:

"My doctor recently told me that jogging could add years to my life. I think he was right. I feel 10 years older already."

RODNEY DANGERFIELD
comedian:

"The trouble with jogging is that by the time you realize you're in shape for it, it's too far to walk back."
   (Also attributed to comedian Marty Allen)

MIKE ROYKO
sportswriter:

"It's unnatural for people to run around city streets unless they are thieves or victims. It makes people nervous to see someone running. I know that when I see somebody running on my street, my instincts tell me to let the dog out after him."

TOM WOLFE
writer:

"Almighty God, as we sail with pure aerobic grace and striped orthotic feet past the blind portals of our fellow citizens, past their chuck roast lives and their necrotic cardiovascular systems and rusting hips and slipped discs and desiccated lungs, past their implacable inertia and inability to persevere and rise above the fully pensioned world they live in and to push themselves to the limits of their capacity and achieve the White Moment of slipping through the Wall, borne aloft on one's Third Wind, past their Cruisomatic cars and upholstered lawn mowers and their gummy-sweet children already at work like

little fat factories producing arterial plaque, the more quickly to join their parents in their joyless bucket-seat landau ride toward the grave—help us, dear Lord, we beseech Thee, as we sail past this cold-lard desolation, to be big about it."

Language

GORDIE HOWE
Hall of Fame hockey player:

"All pro athletes are bilingual. They speak English and profanity."

LOU HOLTZ
Arkansas football coach:

"The Good Lord allows just so much profanity on a team, and I use up our entire quota."

DIZZY DEAN
major league pitcher-turned-broadcaster, in response to urgings by the St. Louis board of education that he be relieved of his broadcasting duties with the Cardinals because of his atrocious grammar:

"A lot of folks that ain't saying 'ain't' ain't eating."

JIM MURRAY
sportswriter:

"Casey Stengel is a white American male with a speech pattern that ranges somewhere between the sound a porpoise makes underwater and an Abyssinian rug merchant."

ROD DEDEAUX
University of Southern California baseball coach:

"I always understood everything Casey Stengel said, which sometimes worried me."

JEAN CRUGUET
French-born jockey:

"When I first came here, I worked the Florida tracks. It's hard to learn English when everybody is speaking Spanish."

TOM COUSINEAU
Ohio State linebacker who spurned the NFL to play in Canada:

"I wish I'd have paid more attention in French classes. The first time I ordered prime rib in a restaurant, I got hamburger."

JOE E. LOUIS
comedian:

"I read the French racing paper, but the horses seem to lose in the translation."

FRESCO THOMPSON
Brooklyn Dodgers scout, reporting on weak-hitting French-Canadian minor league outfielder Paul Merrinow:

"He's thinking in French and they're pitching to him in English."

CHI CHI RODRIGUEZ
Puerto Rican professional golfer, on his accent:

"It's still embarrassing. I asked my caddie for a sand wedge, and 10 minutes later he came back with a ham on rye."

TOMMY LASORDA
Los Angeles Dodgers manager, on Fernando Valenzuela during the pitcher's 1982 holdout:

"All last year we tried to teach him English, and the only word he learned was 'million.' "

DIZZY DEAN
major league pitcher-turned-broadcaster, explaining *spart*, a word he frequently used in his broadcasts:

"Spart is pretty much like gumption or fight. Like the Spart of St. Louis, that plane Lindbergh flowed to Europe."

GEORGE CHEMERES
boxing promoter, explaining a term he uses:

"You know, a half-a-David is one of those legal papers you prove things with."

DIZZY DEAN
major league pitcher-turned-broadcaster, in response to schoolteachers' criticism of his grammar:

"You learn 'em English and I'll learn 'em baseball."

Life

SIR WALTER SCOTT
Scottish writer:

"Life is itself but a game of football."

JOE FRAZIER
heavyweight boxing champion:

"Life don't run away from nobody. Life runs at people."

LOU HOLTZ
Arkansas football coach:

"One day you are drinking the wine, and the next day you are picking the grapes."

WALTER HAGEN
professional golfer, on how to live:

"Don't hurry. Don't worry. You're only here on a short visit, so don't forget to stop and smell the flowers."

JOE SCHMIDT
Detroit Lions coach:

"Life is a shit sandwich, and every day you take another bite."

EMIL ZATOPEK
Czechoslovakian Olympic distance-running champion:

"There are three things worth living for: American luxury, Japanese women and Chinese food."

DAN QUISENBERRY
Kansas City Royals relief pitcher:

"I've seen the future, and it's much like the present, only longer."

MUHAMMAD ALI
heavyweight boxing champion, on how he wishes to be remembered:

"That he took a few cups of love and one teaspoon of patience. One tablespoon of generosity. One pint of kindness. One quart of laughter. Mixed it up and stirred it well. And then he spread it over the span of a lifetime and served it to each and every deserving person he met."

LUIS RODRIGUEZ
boxer:

"My destiny is like my nose. It is something I got from my grandfather. I must protect it. But I can't change it."

WILLIE DAVIS
Mexican League baseball manager and former major league outfielder:

"If you step on people in this life, you're going to come back as a cockroach."

BOB LEMON
major league manager:

"I've come to the conclusion that the two most important things in life are good friends and a good bullpen."

BOB ZUPPKE
Illinois football coach:

"Never let hope elude you. That is life's biggest fumble."

Life on the Road

EARL WEAVER
Baltimore Orioles manager, citing travel demands as a primary factor in his decision to retire:

"What scares the hell out of me is waking up dead some morning in the Hyatt Hotel in Oakland."

PING BODIE
New York Yankees outfielder, asked with whom he was rooming:

"Babe Ruth's valises."

BY SAAM
baseball announcer, refuting the claim that he had a soft job:

"It isn't easy carrying a golf bag around with you on those road trips."

AL HRABOSKY
major league relief pitcher:

"When I'm on the road, my greatest ambition is to get a standing boo."

JEROME WHITEHEAD
Marquette basketball player, after a Brazilian tour:

"It's an unbelievable situation when 25,000 people are booing you and throwing garbage at you. It's like the whole country was Notre Dame."

GEORGE ALLEN
Los Angeles Rams coach:

"The street to obscurity is paved with athletes who performed great feats before friendly crowds. Greatness in major league sports is the ability to win in a stadium filled with people who are pulling for you to lose."

GRAIG NETTLES
New York Yankees third baseman, during an airplane trip:

"We've got a problem. Luis Tiant wants to use the bathroom, and it says no foreign objects in the toilet."

LOU HOLTZ
Arkansas football coach:

"I play as well on the road as I do at home, but my teams don't."

EARL WEAVER
Baltimore Orioles manager, after staying at Pittsburgh's venerable William Penn Hotel during the 1979 World Series:

"I think William Penn may have been named after the hotel, rather than the other way around."

DON SCHOLLANDER
Olympic swimming champion:

"Travel is broadening—especially when you win."

LOU HOLTZ
Arkansas football coach:

"Playing at home is only an advantage if you win. If you lose, you're better off playing on the road, because you have a better chance of getting out of the stadium alive."

Luck

BRANCH RICKEY
major league baseball executive:

"Luck is the residue of design."

SCOTT OSTLER
sportswriter:

"Luck is the residue of luck."

DON SUTTON
major league pitcher:

"Luck is a by-product of busting your fanny."

DARRELL ROYAL
Texas football coach:

"Breaks balance out. The sun don't shine on the same ol' dog's rear end every day."

RED BLAIK
Army football coach:

"Inches make a champion, and the champion makes his own luck."

GEORGE ALLEN
professional football coach:

"The harder I work, the luckier I get."

LANGSTON COLEMAN
Nebraska end:

"It's what you have left over after you give 100 percent."

DARRELL ROYAL
Texas football coach:

"You've got to be in a position for luck to happen. Luck doesn't go around looking for a stumblebum."

DARRELL ROYAL
Texas football coach, on how much good fortune a team can tolerate:

"A little bit of perfume doesn't hurt you if you don't drink it."

LEFTY GOMEZ
Hall of Fame pitcher:

"I'd rather be lucky than good."

GRANTLAND RICE
sportswriter:

Dame Fortune is a cockeyed wench,
  As someone's said before,
And yet the old Dame plays her part
  in any winning score.
Take all the credit you deserve,
  heads-up in winning pride,
But don't forget that Lady Luck
  was riding at your side.

Malapropisms, Mangled Metaphors and Other Curious Phraseologies

DANNY OZARK
Philadelphia Phillies manager:

"I've got a great repertoire with my players."

JERRY COLEMAN
San Diego Padres manager:

"If you ask what the Achilles tendon of the team is, it would be the pitching."

DIZZY DEAN
major league pitcher-turned-broadcaster:

"He's standing confidentially at the plate."

CHICK WERGELS
publicist, on Beau Jack:

"He loves to fight. If he didn't get no pay for it, he'd still wanna fight just to relieve the monopoly."

DANNY OZARK
Philadelphia Phillies manager; asked about his team's morale:

"It's not a question of morality."

YOGI BERRA
New York Yankees catcher:

"[Mickey] Mantle can hit just as good right-handed as he can left-handed. He's just naturally amphibious."

BILL PETERSON
former Florida State football coach, on being selected to the Florida Hall of Fame:

"I'm very appreciative of being indicted."

MICKEY MANTLE
New York Yankees center fielder, testifying before a Senate subcommittee considering antitrust exemptions for baseball immediately after Casey Stengel had exasperated the senators with incomprehensible responses:

"My views are just about the same as Casey's."

BILL LEE
major league pitcher, on the brain's hemispheres:

"You have a left and a right. The left side controls the right half of your body, and the right side controls the left half. Therefore, lefthanders are the only people in their right mind."

155

JOHN MADDEN
sportscaster and former Oakland Raiders coach, on what he told his team before Super Bowl XI:

"I never knew what it meant, but I told the players, 'Don't worry about the horse being blind, just load the wagon.' "

BILL LEE
major league southpaw pitcher:

"A 'flake' is a term created by a right-handed, egotistic, consumeristic, exploitative, non-recycling, carnivorous, right-handed—I've said that, haven't I—population. You get the gist. It couldn't have been a term created by a left hander."

JOHNNY LOGAN
Milwaukee Braves shortstop, after receiving an award:

"I will perish this trophy forever."

MAGIC JOHNSON
Los Angeles Lakers guard:

"I strive on pressure."

JOHNNY LOGAN
Milwaukee Braves shortstop, asked to pick the number-one baseball player of all time:

"I'd have to go with the immoral Babe Ruth."

VINCE FERRAGAMO
Los Angeles Rams quarterback, on oddsmakers' installation of the Rams as a big underdog in Super Bowl XIV:

"How they arrived at their conclusions behooves me."

DANNY OZARK
Philadelphia Phillies manager, after his team blew a 15½-game lead:

"Even Napoleon had his Watergate."

DIZZY DEAN
major league pitcher-turned-broadcaster:

"The runners have returned to their respectable bases."

MARTINA NAVRATILOVA
professional tennis player:

"That's no hair off my chest."

JACK KRAFT
Villanova basketball coach, on losing a key player who fouled out in the waning minutes of a close game:

"That was the nail that broke the coffin's back."

LEFTY PHILLIPS
California Angels manager, after a tough loss:

"It's all water under the dam."

LEFTY PHILLIPS
California Angels manager:

"Our phenoms ain't phenomenating."

JERRY COLEMAN
San Diego Padres broadcaster:

"There's a fly to deep center field. Winfield is going back, back. He hits his head against the wall! It's rolling toward second base!"

JOHNNY LOGAN
Milwaukee Braves shortstop, upon being introduced to someone:

"I know the name, but I can't replace the face."

FRED WHITE
Kansas City Royals broadcaster, reading a wire-service summary that mistakenly showed the same starter and relief pitcher for the Minnesota Twins:

"Well, I see in the game in Minnesota that Terry Felton has relieved himself on the mound in the second inning."

MAGIC JOHNSON
Los Angeles Lakers guard:

"I only know how to play two ways, and that's reckless and abandon."

YOGI BERRA
New York Yankees catcher, asked one spring what his cap size was:

"How do I know? I'm not in shape yet."

YOGI BERRA
New York Yankees catcher, asked by a waitress whether he'd like his pizza cut into four pieces or eight:

"Better make it four. I don't think I can eat eight."

YOGI BERRA
New York Yankees catcher, when handed a check inscribed "Pay to Bearer":

"This ain't the way to spell my name."

YOGI BERRA
New York Yankees catcher, when his wife told him she had been to see *Doctor Zhivago:*

"Oh, what's the matter with you now?"

YOGI BERRA
New York Yankees catcher, to a woman fan who remarked that he looked cool despite the sweltering heat:

"Thank you, ma'am. You don't look so hot yourself."

YOGI BERRA
New York Yankees catcher, upon seeing Ernest Hemingway in Toots Shor's restaurant and being told he was a writer:

"Yeah? With what paper?"

VINCE FERRAGAMO
Los Angeles Rams quarterback:

"I don't like to look back in retrospect."

JERRY COLEMAN
San Diego Padres broadcaster:

"Rich Folkers is throwing up in the bullpen."

YOGI BERRA
New York Yankees catcher, acknowledging fans on Yogi Berra Day:

"I want to thank everyone who made this day necessary."

DIZZY DEAN
baseball broadcaster:

"Don't fail to miss tomorrow's game."

JOHNNY LOGAN
Milwaukee Braves shortstop:

"Rome wasn't born in a day."

FLOYD SMITH
Toronto Maple Leafs coach, after a loss:

"I've got nothing to say and I'll only say it once."

DARRYL DAWKINS
Philadelphia 76er coach, before taking a vow of silence with sportswriters:

"Nothing means nothing, but it isn't really nothing because nothing is something that isn't."

VINCE FERRAGAMO
Los Angeles Rams quarterback, on coach Ray Malavasi:

"He never relinquishes my disbelief."

JOHNNY LOGAN
Milwaukee Braves shortstop:

"I'll have pie à la mode with ice cream."

CASEY STENGEL
New York Yankees manager:

"Good pitching will always stop good hitting, and vice versa."

DIZZY DEAN
St. Louis Cardinals pitcher, after being hit in the head by a baseball in the 1934 World Series:

"The doctors x-rayed my head and found nothing."

MARK SNOW
New Mexico basketball player:

"Strength is my biggest weakness."

YOGI BERRA
New York Yankees catcher, on Toots Shor's restaurant in New York:

"It's so crowded nobody goes there anymore."

JERRY COLEMAN
San Diego Padres broadcaster:

   "He slides into second with a stand-up double."

HOWARD COSELL
sportscaster:

   "Let us reflect back nostalgically on the past."

CASEY STENGEL
New York Mets manager, referring to a former colleague:

   "He's dead at the present time."

YOGI BERRA
New York Yankees catcher, on why shadowy left field at Yankee Stadium
is tough on fielders during late-season day games:

   "It gets late early out there."

PHIL WATSON
professional hockey player, to the press:

   "Gentlemen, I have nothing to say. Any questions?"

DANNY OZARK
Philadelphia Phillies manager:

   "I will not be co-horsed."

HARVEY KUENN
Milwaukee Brewers manager, after the Brewers rallied from two games
down to beat the California Angels in the 1982 American League playoffs:

   "They had us with the walls to our back."

WES WESTRUM
New York Mets manager, after the Mets rallied with two outs in the ninth
for a victory:

   "Now, gentlemen, that was a cliff-dweller to end all cliff-dwellers."

CASEY STENGEL
New York Yankees manager, to a group of rookies assembled for spring
training:

   "Now all you fellers line up alphabetically by height."

YOGI BERRA
New York Yankees catcher:

   "If people don't want to come out to the park, nobody's gonna stop
'em."

YOGI BERRA
New York Yankees catcher, setting
aside his comic book to converse with
teammate Bobby Brown, who had
been reading *Gray's Anatomy:*

"How did yours come out?"

JOE KUHARICH
Philadelphia Eagles coach:

"Trading quarterbacks is rare, but not unusual."

LABRON HARRIS, JR.
PGA tournament official, on rescheduling the Bob Hope Desert Classic
from February to January:

"We think it has a much better chance to be as good as always."

DIZZY DEAN
St. Louis Cardinals pitcher, prior to the 1934 World Series between the
Cards and Detroit:

"This series is already won, but I don't know by which team."

BILL PETERSON
Florida football coach-turned-sportscaster:

"This is the greatest country in America."

BILL WHITE
baseball broadcaster, after New York Yankees outfielder Dave Winfield
reached into the outfield stands to catch a ball hit by Oakland's Tony
Armas in the second game of the 1981 American League playoffs:

"Winfield robbed Armas of at least a home run."

JOHNNY WALKER
middleweight wrist-wrestling champion, on the nature of his sport:

"It's about 90 percent strength and 40 percent technique."

OTTO GRAHAM
former Cleveland Browns quarterback, in an interview just before the
Browns and the Cincinnati Bengals met for the second time ever:

"It will be a typical Browns–Bengals game."

MAGIC JOHNSON
Los Angeles Lakers forward:

"It's really great being Magic Johnson the basketball player for eight
months and then just plain Earvin Johnson for the other three."

PAUL GUANZON
sportscaster, asked on a radio talk show how one breaks into his profession:

"It's not politics, it's just who you know."

DANNY OZARK
Philadelphia Phillies manager:

"Half this game is 90 percent mental."

Marriage and Divorce

PAUL HORNUNG
Green Bay Packers running back:

"Never get married in the morning, 'cause you never know who you'll meet that night."

DR. JOYCE BROTHERS
psychologist whose husband is a sports addict:

"If we did get a divorce, the only way he would know it is if they would announce it on *Wide World of Sports.*"

BILLY TUBBS
Oklahoma basketball coach, on being the second choice for the job:

"It doesn't bother me. I was also my wife's second choice, and we've been married 25 years."

OSCAR LEVANT
pianist and composer, on the divorce of Joe DiMaggio and Marilyn Monroe:

"It proves that no man can be a success in two national pastimes."

MUHAMMAD ALI
heavyweight boxing champion:

"Everybody says they'll marry till death, and they're divorced a few weeks later. I've lied to the judge twice myself."

SATCHEL PAIGE
Cleveland Indians pitcher, asked by club owner Bill Veeck if he was married:

"No, sir, but I'm in great demand."

DON SIKES
professional golfer:

"When I come back in the next life, I want to come back as a golf pro's wife. She wakes up every morning at the crack of ten and is faced by her first major decision of the day: whether to have breakfast in bed or in the hotel coffee shop."

JOHN MCKAY
Tampa Bay Buccaneers coach:

"It's only natural for players who aren't starting to be unhappy. Everyone is unhappy at times, even my wife. Only, she doesn't get interviewed about it."

BOBBY HULL
Hall of Fame hockey player, on his divorce:

"My wife made me a millionaire. I used to have three million."

MARY HENSON
wife of Illinois basketball coach Lou Henson, amid criticism of her husband for his substituting patterns:

"Dear, you just make all the substitutions you want. Just don't carry it over into your personal life."

CORKY MCKAY
wife of Tampa Bay Buccaneers coach John McKay:

"I've spent my life watching stadium clocks that run either too fast or too slow."

HAZEL WEISS
wife of New York Yankees general manager George Weiss, upon her husband's forced retirement:

"I married him for better or worse, but not for lunch."

ANNE HAYES
wife of Ohio State football coach Woody Hayes, asked whether she had ever considered divorce:

"Divorce? No. Murder? Yes."

PEPPER RODGERS
college football coach:

"I had only one friend, my dog. My wife was mad at me, and I told her a man ought to have at least two friends. She agreed—and bought me another dog."

BILLIE JEAN KING
professional tennis player:

"Marriage isn't a 50-50 proposition very often. It's more like 100–0 one moment and 0–100 the next."

LEE TREVINO
professional golfer:

"My wife doesn't care what I do when I'm away—as long as I don't enjoy myself."

JIMMY PIERSALL
major league outfielder and father of 10, on how to pin diapers:

"You cross first base over to third and home plate over to second."

TUG MCGRAW
Philadelphia Phillies relief pitcher:

"I met my wife in a New York bar. We had a lot in common. We were both from California and we were both drunk."

BUM PHILLIPS
Houston Oilers coach:

"I take my wife with me everywhere because she is too ugly to kiss good-bye."

PAUL HORNUNG
Green Bay Packers running back, on why his marriage ceremony was before noon:

"Because if it didn't work out, I didn't want to blow the whole day."

RAY PERKINS
New York Giants football coach, asked whether his wife minded his 18-hour workdays:

"I don't know. I don't see her that much."

DON JAMES
Washington football coach, on why he's grateful for *Playboy* magazine's annual "Pigskin Preview":

"It's the only time of the year my wife lets me buy the magazine. But she reminds me that *Playboy* is a lot like *National Geographic.* Both have pictures of places I'm never going to visit."

ANNE HAYES
wife of Ohio State football coach Woody Hayes, in response to a heckler who said "Your husband is a fathead!":

"What husband isn't?"

DUFFY DAUGHERTY
former Michigan State football coach, recalling his glory days:

"When I got home my wife always had my robe, slippers and hot water waiting for me. She hated for me to wash the dishes in cold water."

LARRY BROWN
New Jersey Nets coach, on his wife, Barbara:

"She's an amateur tennis player and a professional shopper."

LONNIE NICHOLS
Oklahoma City University basketball coach, acknowledging he spends long hours away from home:

"Bless my wife's heart. She grew up as an only child, and she thinks she still is."

Martial Arts

DR. HAROLD E. KENNEY
former Illinois wrestling coach:

"It's a form of Oriental offensive grunting. If a man using karate has laryngitis, he is disarmed."

MIKE ANDERSON
contact karate promoter:

"People don't want to see touch football. They want to see two guys knock the crap out of each other."

JIM MURRAY
sportswriter, on judo's ceremonial traditions:

"Just after you have been slammed to the ground in front of a crowd, you are expected to stand at attention and bow gravely to your opponent as if he had just handed you a plate of fortune cookies and tea."

Monday Morning Quarterbacks

ALEX AGASE
Purdue football coach:

"If you really want to advise me, do it on Saturday afternoon between one and four o'clock. And you've got 25 seconds to do it, between plays. Not on Monday. I know the right thing to do on Monday."

JIM TATUM
North Carolina football coach:

"When I go to bed after losing a game and lie there wondering why I didn't pass or kick or run under such and such a condition, I know that 20,000 other people are in their beds wondering about just that very thing, too. I tell you, it's a great feeling of fellowship."

KNUTE ROCKNE
Notre Dame football coach, asked after a game why Notre Dame had lost:

"I won't know until my barber tells me on Monday."

Money

DR. FERDIE PACHECO
boxing physician, on the sale of video cassettes showing both Muhammad Ali–Leon Spinks fights for $89.95:

"Hell, for that money Spinks will come to your house."

ILIE NASTASE
professional tennis player, explaining why he didn't report the loss of his American Express credit card:

"Whoever stole it is spending less money than my wife."

LARRY BIRD
Boston Celtics forward:

"I really don't like talking about money. All I can say is that the Good Lord must have wanted me to have it."

TICKY BURDEN
Utah guard, on what he would do with the big money he might receive in the pros:

"Live in it, drive it, wear it and eat it."

SAM RUBIN
owner of thoroughbred John Henry, a prodigious winner:

"One of these days John Henry's going to ask me what I've done with all his money."

RULY CARPENTER
Philadelphia Phillies owner:

"I'm going to write a book—*How to Make a Small Fortune in Baseball.* You start with a *large* fortune."

JOHNNY MILLER
professional golfer, on the big money available on the pro tour:

"The dollars aren't so important—once you have them."

CHUCK TANNER
major league baseball manager:

"You can have money stacked to the ceiling, but the size of your funeral is still going to depend upon the weather."

BILL FITCH
Boston Celtics coach:

"I'm independently wealthy. I have enough money to last me the rest of my life—provided I die tomorrow."

WALTER HAGEN
former professional golfer:

"I never wanted to be a millionaire. I just wanted to live like one."

DAVE EICHELBERGER
professional golfer, after accepting a tournament check for $7,200:

"One more like that and I'll be up to broke."

LEE TREVINO
professional golfer:

"There are no rich Mexicans. They get some money, they call themselves Spanish."

DAVID THOMPSON
North Carolina State basketball player, after resisting offers to turn pro before using up his college eligibility:

"You can wear only one suit at a time, drive one car and eat just three meals a day. What do I need with a million dollars?"

WILLIE MAYS
Hall of Fame outfielder:

"The financial careers of most professional athletes can be summed up in these words: short and sweet—but mostly short."

DOUG SANDERS
former professional golfer:

"I'm working as hard as I can to get my life and my cash to run out at the same time. If I can just die after lunch Tuesday, everything will be perfect."

EDWARD BENNETT WILLIAMS
Baltimore Orioles owner:

"I believe there are certain things that cannot be bought: loyalty, friendship, health, love and an American League pennant."

PHIL LINZ
major league baseball utilityman:

"You can't get rich sitting on the bench—but I'm giving it a try."

ROGER KAHN
writer, on Brooklyn Dodgers executive Branch Rickey:

"He had a Puritan distaste for money in someone else's hands."

DAVE HERSH
Portland Beavers general manager, after having newly signed Luis Tiant undergo a medical examination:

"The doctor called and told me Luis was in excellent financial condition."

CHUCK CONNORS
actor and former Brooklyn Dodger, on Dodgers executive Branch Rickey:

"He had both players and money—and just didn't like to see the two of them mix."

DARRELL WALTRIP
stock-car racer, after receiving a $10,000 check at a New York luncheon for being NASCAR driver of the year:

"I appreciate the $10,000 very much. It would last me a year back home in Franklin [Tenn.], but it may not get me through the afternoon up here."

BUM PHILLIPS
Houston Oilers coach, after locker room thieves stole $7,000 in money and jewelry from the team's coaches:

"Evidently the robbers don't know that the players make more than the coaches do. They picked on the wrong guys."

LAMAR HUNT
sports entrepreneur, on his luxurious offices:

"We gave the interior decorator an unlimited budget and he exceeded it."

BILL RUSSELL
former Boston Celtics center, on why he worries about the future of the NBA:

"Mainly because I got a pension coming."

ELIX PRICE
New Orleans Saints defensive tackle, on why he purchased a disco club in Yazoo City, Mississippi:

"I figured if I was going to be out on the town, I might as well spend money in my own place."

Motivation

BUD WILKINSON
Oklahoma football coach:

"You can motivate players better with kind words than you can with a whip."

HOMER RICE
Cincinnati Bengals coach:

"You can motivate by fear. And you can motivate by reward. But both of those methods are only temporary. The only lasting thing is self-motivation."

DARRELL ROYAL
Texas football coach:

"A head coach is guided by this main objective: dig, claw, wheedle, coax that fanatical effort out of the players. You want them to play every Saturday as if they were planting the flag on Iwo Jima."

KNUTE ROCKNE
Notre Dame football coach:

"An automobile goes nowhere efficiently unless it has a quick, hot spark to ignite things, to set the cogs of the machine in motion. So I try to make every player on my team feel he's the spark keeping our machine in motion. On him depend our success and victories."

VINCE LOMBARDI
NFL coach:

"Coaches who can outline plays on a blackboard are a dime a dozen. The ones who win get inside their players and motivate."

ERNIE BANKS
Chicago Cubs minor league instructor:

"I like my players to be married and in debt. That's the way you motivate them."

VINCE LOMBARDI
Green Bay Packers coach:

"There's nothing that stokes the fire like hate."

VINCE LOMBARDI
Green Bay Packers coach, to his players:

"If you aren't fired with enthusiasm, you'll be fired with enthusiasm."

LOU HOLTZ
Arkansas football coach, on how he motivates offensive linemen:

"I tell them the offensive line is the last stop before the bus stop."

Names

JIM MURRAY
sportswriter:

"When I was a kid back in Connecticut I used to love USC
backfields. You had to be fascinated. I remember rolling the
names off my tongue. Morley Drury. Homer Griffith. Grenville
Landsdell. Gaius Shaver. Irvine Warburton. Orville Mohler.
You read them and felt like going out and throwing rocks at
your mother and father for naming you 'Jim' when they could
have picked something romantic and sturdy like these lucky
guys."

LARRY GUEST
sportswriter:

"A top editor of the Dallas *News* once banned the use of nicknames like 'Tommy,' 'Charlie,' etc. A football writer promptly
reported: 'Doak Walker has been sidelined by a Charles
horse.'"

BILL CALLAHAN
Missouri sports publicist:

"I used to have the worst time remembering names. Then I
took that Sam Carnegie course and I've been all right ever
since."

VITAS GERULAITIS
professional tennis player:

"Everyone thinks my name is Jerry Laitis, and they call me Mr.
Laitis. What can you do when you have a name that sounds like
a disease?"

WOODY HAYES
Ohio State football coach:

"I recruited a Czech kicker, and during the eye examination
the doc asked if he could read the bottom line. The Czech
kicker said, 'Read it! I *know* him!'"

CHRIS BAHR
Oakland Raiders placekicker:

"My wife calls me Much-Maligned. She thinks that's my first name. Every time she reads a story about me, that's always in front of my name."

ERNIE BANKS
former Chicago Cubs first baseman, preparing for a banking career:

"My ultimate dream is to have my own bank, maybe in Paris. I'd call it Banks' Bank on the Left Bank."

JIM ZORN
Seattle Seahawks quarterback, anticipating his first offspring:

"If it's a boy, my neighbors have some friends who want me to name him Bjorn—so the headlines could read 'Bjorn Zorn Born.' "

DIGGER PHELPS
Notre Dame basketball coach, on how he got his nickname:

"My father is an undertaker, and I worked for him part-time. There were certain advantages to the job. For instance, while I was dating my wife I sent her flowers every day."

TOM MOREY
surfer and Boogie Board inventor with sons named Sol, Moon, and Sky, explaining why he abandoned celestial names with his fourth son, Matteson:

"Sky's the limit."

ARA PARSEGHIAN
Notre Dame football coach:

"To pronounce my name you take 'par' as in golf, 'seag' as in Seagram's whiskey, and 'yen' as in Japanese money. Just think of a drunken Japanese golfer."

BOBBY BRAGAN
Milwaukee Braves manager, on catcher Joe Torre:

"I can't understand why he hasn't been nicknamed Chicken. Don't you get it? Chicken Catcher Torre."

CRIS COLLINSWORTH
Cincinnati Bengals receiver:

"Actually, Cris is my middle name. Anthony Cris Collinsworth. [My parents] were going to call me Cris Anthony, but it sounded too much like chrysanthemum."

ALEX KARRAS
Detroit Lions defensive lineman:

"I don't think I would have been much of a football player if I didn't have a name like Karras. That hard 'K' sound is the key. If my name was Harris, an 'H' instead of a 'K,' and they'd baptized me Alexander . . . with *that* name, 'Alexander Harris,' I'd never have made it as a football player—at least not as a defensive tackle. It's not a football player's name. Maybe I could have been a flanker with a name like that . . . but more likely I would have turned out to be the Secretary of the Interior."

JACK CASE
sportswriter, unknowingly tagging boxer Ray Robinson with a nickname:

"This Robinson is as sweet as sugar."

Officials and Officiating

OGDEN NASH,
poet:

> There once was an umpire whose vision
> Was cause for abuse and derision.
> He remarked in surprise,
> "Why pick on my eyes?
> It's my heart that dictates my decision."

BILL MCGOWAN
major league umpire, to a runner who argued vehemently that he was safe at first base:

"If you don't think you're out, read the morning paper."

RON LUCIANO
former major league baseball umpire, on why he's glad to be out of that profession:

"For one thing, now I can wear my glasses when I'm in a restaurant having trouble reading the menu."

BABE MCCARTHY
Memphis Pros basketball coach, objecting to an official's call:

"If that was a foul, I hope the Lord strikes me down right here on the spot. [pause] See, I told you!"

JOE RUE
former major league umpire:

"I've been mobbed, cussed, booed, kicked in the ass, punched in the face, hit with mud balls and whiskey bottles; and had everything from shoes to fruits and vegetables thrown at me . . . An umpire should hate humanity."

RON BOLTON
Cleveland Browns defensive back:

"Officials are the only guys who can rob you and then get a police escort out of the stadium."

TOMMY CANTENBURY
Centenary College basketball coach:

"The trouble with officials is they just don't care who wins."

EARL STROM
NBA referee:

"Officiating is the only occupation in the world where the highest accolade is silence."

NESTOR CHYLAK
major league umpire:

"They expect an umpire to be perfect on opening day and to improve as the season goes on."

(Ed Runge, major league umpire: "It's the only occupation

where a man has to be perfect the first day on the job and then improve over the years."

Lenny Wirtz, NBA referee: "Our job is the only one where you have to start out perfectly and get better each time.")

DOUG HARVEY
major league umpire:

"When I am right, no one remembers. When I am wrong, no one forgets."

ABE LEMONS
college basketball coach:

"You can say something to popes, kings and presidents. But you can't talk to officials. In the next war, they ought to give everybody a whistle."

LARRY GOETZ
major league umpire:

"In a way an umpire is like a woman. He makes quick decisions, never reverses them, and doesn't think you're safe when you're out."

NESTOR CHYLAK
major league umpire:

"This must be the only job in America that everybody knows how to do better than the guy who's doing it."

LARRY GOETZ
major league umpire, explaining to a rookie player why he was ejecting him for arguing:

"I don't mind it when the lions and tigers get on me, but when the nits and gnats get on me, it's too much."

DUSTY BOGGESS
major league umpire, to Chicago Cubs catcher Clyde McCullough, who was complaining that a third strike called on him was a ball:

"You know, Mac, for 20 years as a player I thought that was a ball, too; but it's a strike, so I went to umpiring."

TOMMY GORMAN
former major league umpire:

"Anytime I got those bang-bang plays at first base, I called them out. It made the game shorter."

ADOLPH RUPP
Kentucky basketball coach, protesting a call to an official who also happened to be a state senator:

"Mr. Senator, you can appropriate $73 million to build highways but you can't even recognize a traveling violation when you see it."

PETER SALZBERG
Vermont basketball coach, after officials assessed 56 fouls during a game:

"They called fouls like they were getting a commission."

BOB CONIBEAR
Bowling Green basketball coach, describing his night's sleep after a tough loss in which he was displeased with the officiating:

"I dreamed I was on a safari in Africa and killed every zebra I saw."

DICK ENBERG
sportscaster, recalling his days as a Little League umpire:

"When parents and kids began arguing with me as I walked to my car, I knew $7.50 wasn't enough."

EARL WEAVER
Baltimore Orioles manager, when umpire Ron Luciano signed with NBC as a sportscaster:

"I hope he takes this job more seriously than he did his last one."

SKIP CARAY
sportscaster:

"The only thing tougher than being a basketball referee is being happily married."

Olympic Games

BARON PIERRE DE COUBERTIN
modern Olympic Games founder:

"The important thing in the Olympic Games is not to win but to take part; the important thing in life is not the triumph but the struggle. The essential thing is not to have conquered but to have fought well. To spread these precepts is to build up a stronger and more valiant and, above all, more scrupulous and more gracious humanity."

HOWARD K. SMITH
newscaster:

"We shake our old, untended sports tree every four years and gather whatever plums fall off. Other nations cultivate their orchards day by day, pruning, nursing, root-feeding them and harvesting ever more plums."

DWIGHT STONES
high-jumper, announcing support for the U.S. boycott of the 1980 Summer Olympic Games in Moscow:

"There's something about somebody having a party in their front yard and beating up somebody in their back yard that just doesn't wash with me."

GEORGE E. DANIELSON
chairman of a House subcommittee studying amateur sports, upon learning of the Olympic sport of luge:

"I thought it was something to eat."

Owners and Ownership

RED SMITH
sportswriter:

"Baseball owners have moral scruples against taking any man's dollar when there is a chance to take a dollar and a quarter."

HERMAN SARKOWSKY
Portland Trail Blazers owner:

"Anyone who invests in sports has an ego problem to start with."

JACK BUCK
sportscaster, after seeing New York Yankees principal owner George Steinbrenner's yacht on Tampa Bay:

"It was a beautiful thing to behold, with all 36 oars working in unison."

ART MODELL
Cleveland Browns owner, on the revenue-sharing National Football League owners:

"We're 28 Republicans who vote socialist."

TED TURNER
Atlanta Braves and Hawks owner:

"I never could understand why owners like to sit up behind bulletproof glass sipping martinis. I sit in the front row."

BILL VEECK
Chicago White Sox owner:

"Whatever I've said over the years, the owners have looked at me as though I were a little boy trying to run fast so the propeller on my beanie would spin."

JOHN J. MCMULLEN
former limited partner of New York Yankees owner George Steinbrenner:

"Nothing is more limited than being a limited partner of George's."

DAVE GOLTZ
major league pitcher, on Minnesota Twins owner Calvin Griffith:

"He's the perfect businessman. He likes to get the most for the least. And he likes the least part best."

SAM RUTIGLIANO
Cleveland Browns coach, on the Oakland Raiders owner:

"Al Davis is the kind of guy who would steal your eyes and then try to convince you that you looked better without them."

ROGER VAUGHAN
writer, on Atlanta Braves and Hawks owner Ted Turner's approach to everything he does in life:

"He gets a good hold on the paintbrush, then confidently has the ladder removed."

NED DOYLE
advertising executive, explaining why he was interested in purchasing a franchise in the fledgling American Basketball Association:

"Because the Brooklyn Bridge wasn't for sale."

DAVID H. MCCONNELL
New York millionaire, on why he was interested in purchasing an NFL franchise:

"I could go out and buy 200,000 acres of timberland, but then what would I do? Cheer for the trees?"

JOHN LARDNER
writer, upon hearing of Bill Veeck's purchase of baseball's hapless St. Louis Browns in 1951:

"Many critics were surprised to know that the Browns could be bought because they didn't know the Browns were owned."

GENE AUTRY
Los Angeles Angels owner, on his Dodger counterpart:

"There's nothing in the world I wouldn't do for Walter O'Malley. There's nothing he wouldn't do for me. That's the way it is. We go through life doing nothing for each other."

STEVEN REDDICLIFFE
writer, on Atlanta Braves and Hawks owner Ted Turner:

"The man has mistaken his larynx for a megaphone."

Physical Prowess

REGGIE RUCKER
Cleveland Browns wide receiver, after watching a Hertz television commercial in which O. J. Simpson is shown soaring through the air:

"If this guy can fly, why does he need to rent a car?"

DENISE MCCLUGGAGE
ski instructor:

"Grace is a warmer word for efficiency."

REGGIE WILLIAMS
Cincinnati Bengals linebacker, citing his attributes:

"Speed, strength and the ability to recognize pain immediately."

GARDNER DICKINSON
professional golfer, on the limberness of 69-year-old Sam Snead:

"Sam was born warmed up. If you cut him, 3-In-One oil would come out, not blood."

BOB HANSEN
Iowa basketball player, on playing defense against Louisville's Darrell Griffith:

"I've guarded other guys who could leap high before. But all of them came down."

MIKE DOWNEY
Chicago sportswriter, on Denver Nuggets guard David Thompson:

"The last time anybody jumped like that in Chicago was when Mayor Daley asked an alderman to get him a cup of coffee."

AL MCGUIRE
Marquette basketball coach, on guard Dean Meminger:

"He's as quick as the last mass at a summer resort."

JOSH GIBSON
former Negro leagues outfielder, on teammate James "Cool Papa" Bell:

"Cool Papa Bell was so fast he could get out of bed, turn out the lights across the room and be back in bed under the covers before the lights went out."
    (Also attributed to Muhammad Ali in reference to himself)

CURT GOWDY
sportscaster, on Baltimore Orioles third baseman Brooks Robinson:

"Brooks is not a fast man, but his arms and legs move very quickly."

JIM KILLINGSWORTH
Texas Christian basketball coach, on Tulsa guard Paul Pressey:

"He's quick enough to play tennis by himself."

RALPH KINER
baseball announcer:

"Two-thirds of the earth is covered by water; the other one-third is covered by Garry Maddox."

F. A. DRY,
Texas Christian University football coach, on Southern Methodist University running back Eric Dickerson:

"If he gets two strides on you, the next guy in motion is the scoreboard operator."

LES WOTHKE
Western Michigan basketball coach, on his team:

"We're not real fast. In fact, we had three loose balls roll dead in practice the other day."

BOB CHARLES
professional golfer:

"Being left-handed is a big advantage. No one knows enough about your swing to mess you up with advice."

ROCKY BLEIER
Pittsburgh Steelers balding running back:

"I'd like the body of Jim Brown, the moves of Gale Sayers, the strength of Earl Campbell and the acceleration of O. J. Simpson. And just once I would like to run and feel the wind in my hair."

Physique and Appearance

STEVE TOWLE
Miami Dolphins linebacker, explaining a New Year's resolution:

"Last year I resolved to grow one inch taller and grow hair on my chest. Since neither happened, this year I'm going to hang around with shorter people and keep my shirts buttoned."

PETE ROSE
Cincinnati Reds outfielder, on teammate Wayne Granger:

"He's so skinny the only place he could have won a college letter was Indiana."

GINNY COCO
gymnastics coach, on what a female gymnast should look like:

"You want all the curves in the right places, but not at the level Hugh Hefner might want for the *Playboy* image. Voluptuous girls don't win in gymnastics. You want lean, strong girls, the racehorse type."

PETER VECSEY
sportswriter:

"George McGinnis' hands are so huge I'll bet he's able to palm Sunday."

WAYNE WALKER
former Detroit Lions linebacker, on his baldness:

"Somewhere in Detroit there's a helmet with all my hair in it."

CAROL MANN
professional golfer, on New Orleans Saints coach Bum Phillips' crew cut:

"It reminds me of a good three-wood lie."

LAURA BAUGH
professional golfer noted for her striking good looks:

"When you step on the first tee it doesn't matter what you look like. Being pretty, ugly or semi has no effect on the golf ball. It doesn't help your 5-iron if you're pretty."

JAN STEPHENSON
professional golfer, told that a Dallas sportswriter had rated her a '6':

"I may not be the prettiest girl in the world, but I'd like to see Bo Derek look like a '10' after playing 18 holes of golf in 100-degree heat."

EDDY OTTOZ
Italian hurdler, asked why he competes unshaven:

"Italian men and Russian women never shave before a meet."

BILLIE JEAN KING
5'4½" tennis champion:

"If you're small, you better be a winner."

JIM PALMER
Baltimore Orioles pitcher, on his 5'7" manager Earl Weaver:

"Did you ever notice that Earl always goes to the highest spot on the mound when he comes out?"

MIKE OWENS
teammate of 7'4" basketball center Ralph Sampson at Virginia:

"People keep coming up to Ralph and asking him if he's Ralph Sampson. I mean, who else could he be?"

CHOC HUTCHESON
former sportswriter, on how to solve the Berlin Crisis of the early sixties:

"Induct Big Daddy Lipscomb [288-pound Pittsburgh Steelers defensive lineman] and send him to Berlin in Army fatigues marked 'small.' "

JOE NAMATH
New York Jets quarterback, defending his beard and his hairlength:

"The only perfect man who ever lived had a beard and long hair and didn't wear shoes and slept in barns and didn't hold a regular job and never put on a tie. I'm not comparing myself to Him—I'm in enough trouble trying to stack up against Bart Starr—but I'm just saying that you don't judge a man by the way he cuts his hair."

DARRELL ROYAL
Texas football coach:

"Fat people don't offend me. What offends me is losing with fat people."

BILL VEECK
major league baseball owner, on Eddie Gaedel, the 3′7″ midget he sent to bat for the St. Louis Browns in 1951:

"He'd have been great in a short series."

JIMMY DEMARET
professional golfer, on the young Jack Nicklaus:

"He's like a young Toots Shor—a victim of circumference."

AL HRABOSKY
major league relief pitcher, when asked to shave his facial hair:

"How can I intimidate batters if I look like a goddamn golf pro?"

YOGI BERRA
New York Yankees catcher, recalling spring training of his first full season in the majors:

"Mike Ryba, the Red Sox pitcher . . . had a hobby of picking what he called 'The All-America Ugly Team,' and the first time we went over to Sarasota where the Red Sox trained, he took one look at me and said, 'Kid, I'll have to see you again tomorrow. You must be sick today. Nobody could look that bad unless he was sick.' And then, when he saw me the next day in St. Pete, he said, 'Yogi, I hereby appoint you the captain of the All-Time All-America Ugly Team. You are the ugliest-looking man I ever saw in my whole life.'

"Somebody else spread the gag that I was the only catcher they had ever seen whose looks were improved when he put the mask on."

BILL RUSSELL
former Boston Celtics center:

"The fact that I was a basketball player is incidental, just like the fact I am a person nearly seven feet tall who wears size 15 shoes. I'm just another guy trying to get through life the best I can."

NORMAN RUSSELL
Oklahoma City University basketball player, on the advantages of being seven feet tall:

"You can see Arnold Palmer putt, for one thing."

LYNN SHACKELFORD
UCLA basketball forward-turned-broadcaster, describing the size 22 shoes of Detroit Pistons center Bob Lanier:

"He doesn't shine them—he sends them through a car wash."

MICKEY LOLICH
Detroit Tigers pitcher, on his paunch:

"All the fat guys watch me and say to their wives, 'See? There's a fat guy doing okay. Bring me another beer.'"

BOB FERRY
Baltimore Bullets assistant coach, on seven-footer Lew Alcindor (now Kareem Abdul-Jabbar):

"We're not afraid of him. He puts his pants on the same as we do, except four feet higher."

RON MEYER
Southern Methodist University football coach, on his 5'9", 220-pound guard Harvey McAtee:

"He's so short his breath smells of earthworms."

DON BEAUPRE
Minnesota North Stars 5'8", 149-pound goalie, bristling at repeated references to his size:

"I only have to stop the puck, not beat it to death."

ANONYMOUS FAN
to former NFL coach John Madden in reference to his appearance in a popular TV commercial:

"If you got that way drinking Miller Lite, I'd hate to see Miller Heavy."

LOU HOLTZ
Arkansas football coach, recalling when his wife once teased him about how skinny he is:

"That hurt, but I quickly reminded her that a small defect like that kept me from getting a more beautiful wife."

ROOSEVELT GRIER
Los Angeles Rams 300-pound tackle, asked if he had a middle initial:

"No, but I've never been mistaken for anyone else."

JIM MURRAY
sportswriter, on seven-foot-plus basketball center Wilt Chamberlain:

"Sir Edmund Hillary was introduced to Wilt and promptly organized an expedition to climb it. . . ."

Plaudits

JIM MURRAY
sportswriter:

"Bill Russell is a great defensive player, but what he does under the basket is as hard to see as Texas chiggers—as Bill intends."

ARTHUR "BUGS" BAER
sportswriter, on Lefty Grove, who once struck out Babe Ruth, Lou Gehrig and Bob Meusel with nine pitches:

"He could throw a lamb chop past a wolf."

JOHNNY FREDERICK
Brooklyn Dodgers outfielder, on pitcher Dazzy Vance:

"He could throw a cream puff through a battleship."

JOE ADCOCK
Milwaukee Braves first baseman:

"Trying to sneak a pitch past Hank Aaron is like trying to sneak the sunrise past a rooster."

MERV RETTENMUND
major league outfielder, asked if he'd rather face Jim Palmer or Tom Seaver:

"That's like asking if I'd rather be hung or go to the electric chair."

REGGIE JACKSON
major league outfielder, on Tom Seaver:

"Blind people come to the park just to listen to him pitch."

LEE ALLEN
baseball historian, on Babe Ruth:

"For almost two decades he battered fences with such regularity that baseball's basic structure was eventually pounded into a different shape."

JIM FREY
Kansas City Royals manager, on George Brett:

"He could hit buckshot with barbed wire."

TIM MCCARVER
longtime battery mate of pitcher Steve Carlton:

"Carlton does not pitch to the hitter, he pitches through him. The batter hardly exists for Steve. He's playing an elevated game of catch."

KYLE ROTE
New York Giants captain, on the versatility of teammate Frank Gifford:

"Gifford does so many things well that he's put more men out of work than Eli Whitney."

JOHN MCKAY
University of Southern California football coach, on Bear Bryant:

"When you scrape away all the hayseed, you find you're looking at the royal flush underneath. You can beat the Bear once, but never the same way twice."

BUM PHILLIPS
Houston Oilers coach, on Miami Dolphins coach Don Shula:

"He can take his'n and beat your'n, or he can take your'n and beat his'n."

BILL FITCH
Cleveland Cavaliers coach:

"Going into a game against Lew Alcindor is like going into a knife fight and finding there's no blade in your handle."

DOUGLAS MACARTHUR
Army five-star general, on Ty Cobb:

"This great athlete seems to have understood early in his professional career that in the competition of baseball, just as in war, defensive strategy never has produced ultimate victory, and as a consequence, he maintained an offensive posture to the end of his baseball days."

JIMMY CANNON
sportswriter, on heavyweight boxing champion Joe Louis:

"He's a credit to his race—the human race."

ARCHIE MOORE
former light heavyweight boxing champion, on his manager Doc Kearns:

"Give Doc 100 pounds of steel wool and he'd knit you a stove."

BUM PHILLIPS
Houston Oilers coach, on running back Earl Campbell:

"He may not be in a class by himself, but whatever class he's in, it doesn't take long to call roll."

BOBBY MURCER
major league outfielder:

"Trying to hit Phil Niekro is like trying to eat Jell-O with chopsticks."

DOAK WALKER
former Detroit Lions halfback, on his old high school buddy and former Lions teammate, Hall of Fame quarterback Bobby Layne:

"Bobby never lost a game in his life. Time just ran out on him."

BOBBY JONES
golf's only "Grand Slam" winner, after Jack Nicklaus' masterly victory at the 1965 Masters:

"[Arnold] Palmer and [Gary] Player played superbly. But Nicklaus played a game with which I'm not familiar."

JIM MURRAY
sportswriter, on Hall of Fame baseball executive Branch Rickey:

"He could recognize a great player from the window of a moving train."

JIM FREY
Kansas City Royals manager:

"George Brett could get good wood on an aspirin."

Player Draft

GIL BRANDT
Dallas Cowboys chief scout, on the use of computers in drafting:

"I'll say one thing for them—they never try to sell you their brother-in-law as a prospect."

RAY SCOTT
Detroit Pistons coach, asked which NBA team was hurt most by the 1974 expansion draft that stocked the New Orleans franchise:

"New Orleans."

JOHN THOMPSON
Seattle Seahawks general manager, after drafting UCLA's Manu Tuiasosopo:

"We changed our philosophy a little this year. Instead of taking the best athlete, we took the best Samoan."

COTTON FITZSIMMONS
Kansas City Kings coach, on why he wasn't interested in drafting Indiana State All-American Larry Bird:

"I already have two white guys on my team."

SAMMY BAUGH
New York Titans football coach, in response to owner Harry Wismer's advice to ignore the player draft and instead obtain players cut from other teams:

"There's no way you can win games by using people who aren't good enough to make the teams you're trying to beat."

DENNIS HARRISON
Philadelphia Eagles defensive end, on why he wasn't drafted until the fourth round:

"The scouts said I looked like Tarzan and played like Jane."

Players of Today

DARRELL ROYAL
Texas football coach in 1973:

"The trouble with making comparisons in the way people act from one generation to the next is that humans are the most forgetful species on earth. I see only one big difference in football players today. More of them write books."

BOB LEMON
major league baseball manager in 1981:

"Today's players like to play their stereos early because after the game their hair dryers cause static."

BOBBY HULL
Hall of Fame hockey player in 1974:

"Why should a guy with a half-million-dollar contract want to have blood dripping down his face? Or sweat? Or play with bruises? Hell, they won't even play with bruised feelings now."

TY COBB
Detroit Tigers outfielder, in 1925:

"The great trouble with baseball today is that most of the players are in the game for the money that's in it—not for the love of it, the excitement of it and the thrill of it. Times seem to have changed since I broke in more than a generation ago. I really believe that in those days, if a player had been forced to choose between a 50-percent cut in pay or complete retirement from the game, he would have taken the cut—and gladly."

JOHNNY KERR
NBA coach, on players of the seventies:

"They know the latest dance steps, but they don't know the plays."

Playing Conditions

RED SMITH
sportswriter, on the 1963 NFL championship game between New York and Chicago:

"It was an ideal day for football—too cold for the spectators and too cold for the players."

HENRY JORDAN
Green Bay Packers defensive tackle, on the 13-below-zero temperature that prevailed at the start of the Packers' 1967 NFL championship game against the Dallas Cowboys:

"Lombardi got down on his hands and knees and prayed for cold and he stayed down too long."

NORMAN MAILER
writer, on the disadvantages of artificial turf on football fields:

"The injuries are brutal and the fields stink; at the end of the game they smell of vomit and spit and blood because it doesn't go into the earth. All the odors just cook there on this plastic turf."

DAN QUISENBERRY
major league pitcher:

"Natural grass is a wonderful thing for little bugs and sinkerball pitchers."

TUG MCGRAW
major league pitcher, asked whether he favors grass or AstroTurf:

"I don't know. I never smoked AstroTurf."

RICHIE ALLEN
St. Louis Cardinals slugger, and a horseman, on artificial playing surfaces:

"If a horse can't eat it, then I don't like it."

EMILE FRANCIS
New York Rangers coach and general manager, on the rink in Madison Square Garden:

"I've seen better ice on the roads in Saskatchewan."

GENE SARAZEN
professional golfer, describing the course at Congressional Country Club in anticipation of the 1964 U.S. Open:

"The fairways are so narrow the player and his caddie will have to walk them Indian file."

BOB ROSBURG
professional golfer, on the Hazeltine National Golf Club at Chaska, Minnesota, with its 10 dogleg holes:

"Robert Trent Jones must have laid out the course in a kennel."

SAM RUTIGLIANO
Cleveland Browns coach, on whether frigid temperatures contributed to a fumble-marred loss to Cincinnati:

"I checked everybody before the game and they were all 98.6."

PAUL BROWN
Cleveland Browns coach, on why the shotgun offense is not favored in the Midwest, where teams frequently play in mud and freezing temperatures:

"Under those conditions, I doubt if the shotgun would go off."

LEE TREVINO
professional golfer, on why he disdains foul-weather tournaments:

"I can't swing the way I want to with four sweaters and my pajamas and a rain jacket on."

ANONYMOUS
English tennis official:

"If God had meant Wimbledon to be played in great weather, he would have put it in Acapulco."

JERRY TARKANIAN
University of Nevada, Las Vegas basketball coach, on preparing for games at Wyoming (elevation 7,165 feet):

"I try to tell our guys that the altitude isn't that bad because we're playing indoors."

Prayer

CHUCK MILLS
Wake Forest football coach:

"Some coaches pray for wisdom. I pray for 260-pound tackles."

DON CHERRY
Boston Bruins coach:

"When I said my prayers as a kid, I'd tell the Lord I wanted to be a pro hockey player. Unfortunately, I forgot to mention National Hockey League, so I spent 16 years in the minors."

DUFFY DAUGHERTY
Michigan State football coach:

"All those football coaches who hold dressing-room prayers before a game should be forced to attend church once a week."

JOHN McKAY
Tampa Bay Buccaneers coach, asked if his teams pray for victory:

"God's busy. They have to make do with me."

Preparation and Conditioning

CUS D'AMATO
fight manager:

"The hardest thing about fight managing is preparing a fighter for a match. You can get him 80 percent ready, or 85 percent, but you can't get him 100 percent ready. Because if a fighter goes into that ring 100 percent prepared and he loses, he has no excuse."

RED BLAIK
Army football coach, justifying his tough contact practices:

"You don't develop good teeth by eating mush."

DICK GORDON
Apollo 12 astronaut:

"Preparing for a flight into space is much like an athlete's training, except that it takes a bit longer. We train three years for one ball game, and there are only 50 players to begin with; and some don't get in the game."

POP WARNER
college football coach:

"You play the way you practice."

BRUCE JENNER
Olympic decathlon champion, on the difference between him and Joe Namath:

"I spent 12 years training for a career that was over in a week. Joe spent a week training for a career that lasted 12 years."

G. K. CHESTERTON
English writer:

"A man must love a thing very much if he not only practises it without any hope of fame and money, but even practises it without any hope of doing it well."

MIKE REID
Cincinnati Bengals lineman and excellent pianist:

"If I prepared for a concert the way I prepare for a football game, I would begin by throwing the piano out the window."

GRANTLAND RICE
sportswriter:

You wonder how they do it and you look to
   see the knack,
You watch the foot in action, or the shoulder,
   or the back,
But when you spot the answer where the
   higher glamours lurk,
You'll find in moving higher up the
   laurel covered spire,
That the most of it is practice and the
   rest of it is work.

(from "How to Be a Champion")

ABE LEMONS
Texas basketball coach:

"One day of practice is like one day of clean living. Doesn't do you any good."

ED MACAULEY
professional basketball player:

"When you are not practicing, remember, someone somewhere is practicing, and when you meet him he will win."

ROCKY MARCIANO
heavyweight boxing champion:

"I have always adhered to two principles. The first one is to train hard and get into the best possible physical condition. The second is to forget all about the other fellow until you face him in the ring and the bell sounds for the fight."

DR. DANIEL HANLEY
U.S. Olympic team physician:

"By itself, practice does not make perfect. Those of us with a 10-year-old son practicing the trumpet may understand that."

PEPPER MARTIN
St. Louis Cardinals third baseman/outfielder:

"You can take an ol' mule and run him and feed him and train him and get him in the best shape of his life, but you ain't going to win the Kentucky Derby."

GAIL GOODRICH
Los Angeles Lakers guard, on what happens after the team's 10:00 A.M. practice on non-game days:

"We go back to the motel and wake up Wilt."

DAN FAMBROUGH
Kansas football coach:

"You can't really tell anything from spring practice. It's like having your daughter come in at four o'clock in the morning with a Gideon Bible."

ALEX KARRAS
Detroit Lions defensive tackle, on preparing for games:

"A lot of it is psychological. I tell myself before a game that I'm Paul Bunyan. I wake up in the hotel room in the morning and say to myself, 'Paul, we're going to have ourselves a game this afternoon. We are going to remove the stuffings from people.' I can feel myself inflate."

JOHNNY SAIN
major league pitcher, disputing the adage that running is essential to a pitcher's conditioning:

"You don't run the damn ball across the plate."

(Art Fowler, Philadelphia Phillies pitcher: "Heck, if running were so important, Jesse Owens would be a 20-game winner."

Luis Tiant, New York Yankees pitcher: "How many 20-game seasons has Jesse Owens got?")

BOB JOHNSON
Southern Methodist University hurdler, on why he never got started on a weight-lifting program:

"I've been trying to, but I can't get them out of my car."

DON HUTSON
Green Bay Packers receiver:

"For every pass I ever caught in a game, I caught a thousand in practice."

JOHN LOWENSTEIN
Baltimore Orioles designated hitter, on how he stays ready:

"I flush the john between innings to keep my wrists strong."

CHUCK NOLL
Pittsburgh Steelers coach:

"The most interesting thing about this sport, at least to me, is the activity of preparation—any aspect of preparing for the games. The thrill isn't in the winning, it's in the doing."

The Press

H. L. MENCKEN
editor/writer:

"I know of no subject, save perhaps baseball, on which the average American newspaper discourses without unfailing sense and understanding."

EARL WARREN
Chief Justice of the United States:

"I always turn to the sports page first. The sports page records people's accomplishments; the front page nothing but man's failure."

GERALD R. FORD
thirty-eighth President of the United States:

"I'd rather be on the sports page than on the front page."

MARTINA NAVRATILOVA
professional tennis player:

"In Czechoslovakia there is no such thing as freedom of the press. In the United States there is no such thing as freedom from the press."

EKHARDT KRAUTZUN
Fort Lauderdale Strikers soccer team coach:

"I don't care what they say in the papers about me, as long as it isn't true."

JOE DIMAGGIO
New York Yankees outfielder, on his early unworldliness:

"I can remember a reporter asking for a quote, and I didn't know what a quote was. I thought it was some kind of a soft drink."

TOM FORMAN
half of the Forman & Templeton team that produces "The Sporting Life" comics, on how neighbors view him and his partner:

"They're very suspicious. All they know about us is that we work for a syndicate, get phone calls from New York, never go out and have meetings in the basement."

JOHNNY LOGAN
Milwaukee Braves shortstop, when informed that a mistake in the Milwaukee *Journal* that he had complained about was a typographical error:

"The hell it was. It was a clean base hit."

TOMMY LASORDA
Los Angeles Dodgers manager:

"I read every [newspaper] I can get my hands on from front to back. And in the business I'm in, that includes the classifieds for unemployment."

AL DAVIS
Oakland Raiders owner, on Pete Rozelle:

"If Richard Nixon had had Pete Rozelle's publicity staff, he still would be President."

Pressure

LEE TREVINO
professional golfer:

"Anytime you play golf for whatever you've got, that's pressure. I'd like to see H. L. Hunt go out there and play for $3 billion."

BILL LEE
Montreal Expos relief pitcher, asked during the late stages of a pennant race how much pressure he was feeling:

"Thirty-two pounds per square inch at sea level."

LEE TREVINO
professional golfer:

"We all choke, and the man who says he doesn't choke is lying like hell. We all leak oil."

VINCE LOMBARDI
Washington Redskins coach, defending his demanding coaching tactics:

"If they can't put up with my pressure, how are they ever going to stand the pressure from 60,000 people?"

AL MCGUIRE
Marquette basketball coach, defining a pressure game:

"It's when you look at a cheerleader and don't notice her body."

LEE TREVINO
professional golfer:

"You don't know what pressure is until you play for five bucks with only two in your pocket."

Pro Sports

AVERY BRUNDAGE
United States Olympic Committee president:

"Professional sports should be reported on the entertainment pages along with circuses and vaudeville."

BOB COUSY
Cincinnati Royals coach:

"I like the purity of the pros. They tell everybody that they want to win and make money, and that's what they do."

BOBBY KNIGHT
Indiana basketball coach, asked if he would consider coaching in the NBA:

"Hell, I don't even watch the pros. If the NBA was on Channel 5 and a bunch of frogs making love were on Channel 4, I'd watch the frogs—even if they came in fuzzy."

JOHN WOODEN
former UCLA basketball coach, on why he dislikes pro basketball:

"It's great if you want to watch individual play, but I like *team* play. . . . The lack of hustle and thinking bothers me on some pro teams. Heck, if I want to watch great individual play, I'll watch golf or track."

BILL WALTON
Portland Trail Blazers center, on his biggest problem upon entering professional basketball:

"Deciding what to do with my free time."

Public Speaking

BLACKIE SHERROD
Sportswriter, beginning his remarks at a Texas Hall of Fame luncheon:

"I am indeed grateful for this opportunity to rise and welcome you, particularly since I have always admired greatly the men being inducted into the Hall of Fame, since two great teams—Syracuse and Texas—are present, and also since the program is long and this is the last chance to straighten my shorts."

ARCHIE MOORE,
former light heavyweight boxing champion, on why he prefers speaking at prisons:

"Because nobody walks out in the middle of my speech."

ANNE HAYES
wife of Ohio State football coach Woody Hayes:

"I always say that I am going to talk about sex and marriage, but being a football coach's wife, I don't know much about either."

Putdowns

BRANCH RICKEY
major league baseball executive:

"Leo Durocher is a man with an infinite capacity for immediately making a bad thing worse."

TIM KRUMRIE
Wisconsin noseguard, to comedian Bob Hope:

"Looks like nobody guarded your nose."

JIMMY DEMARET
former professional golfer, on comedian Bob Hope's golfing ability:

"Bob has a beautiful short game. Unfortunately, it's off the tee."

AL SALVIO
longtime friend of Al McGuire, at a roast honoring the former Marquette basketball coach:

"I knew you when you were just an arrogant, egotistical, pompous athlete from Brooklyn. Now I know you when you're just an arrogant, egotistical, pompous millionaire from Brookfield."

ROCKY BRIDGES
minor league manager, recalling when he batted against Tommy Lasorda in the International League:

"Tommy's curve had a better hang time than Ray Guy's punts."

FRANK HOWARD
Clemson football coach, asked at a coaches' clinic how many great coaches he thought were present:

"One less than [Maryland football coach] Tom Nugent thinks there is."

HARRY KALAS
Philadelphia Phillies announcer, introducing outfielder Garry Maddox at a banquet:

"He's turned his life around. He used to be depressed and miserable. Now he's miserable and depressed."

JIMMY BRESLIN
writer:

"Having Marv Throneberry play for your team is like having Willie Sutton play for your bank."

RICK MONDAY
Los Angeles Dodgers outfielder:

"Mike Ivie is a forty-million-dollar airport with a thirty-dollar control tower."

DOUG DIEKEN
Cleveland Browns tackle, on Cleveland Indians second baseman Duane Kuiper:

"Duane's game reminds me of a lot of bars I go to—all singles and no action."

GARY WILLIAMS
American University basketball coach, after one of his rebounders grabbed just one in 27 minutes of play:

"My nine-year-old daughter could run around out there for 27 minutes and two rebounds would hit her on the head."

JOHN MCKAY
Tampa Bay Buccaneers coach:

"ABC was here last week and shot enough footage for *Gone With the Wind.* After watching the practices, I thought we might be."

LYNDON B. JOHNSON
thirty-sixth President of the U.S., on former Michigan center Gerald R. Ford:

"The trouble with Ford is he played too many years without a helmet."

ANONYMOUS

"The trouble with Gerald Ford is he spent too many years looking at the world upside down and through his legs."

BRANCH RICKEY
major league baseball executive, on the man erroneously credited with
having invented baseball:

"The only thing Abner Doubleday ever started was the Civil War."
(Doubleday aimed the first Union shot in defense of Fort Sumter on
April 12, 1861.)

KAREEM ABDUL-JABBAR
Los Angeles Lakers center, on why he rejected an interview request from
talk-show host Tom Snyder:

"I avoided him because he asks the questions, answers them, and then
comments on the words he puts in your mouth."

SONNY LISTON
heavyweight boxer, to writer Norman Mailer, who asked why Liston had
called him a bum:

"You *are* a bum. I'm a bum, too. I'm just a bigger bum."

RAY MANSFIELD
former Pittsburgh Steelers center, at a roast honoring linebacker Jack
Lambert:

"I taught Jack a lot—how to tie his shoes, how to brush his fangs."

LEE CORSO
Indiana football coach, after his son, Steve, caught a pass against Vanderbilt:

"My wife Betsy could have caught that pass. My mother might have had
a little trouble with it, but Betsy definitely could have caught it."

MUHAMMAD ALI
heavyweight boxing champion, asked how football player Ed "Too Tall"
Jones would fare in his attempt to switch careers and become a boxer:

"Timmmmm-berrrr."

RED SMITH
sportswriter, on the Green Bay Packers' last season before the Vince
Lombardi era:

"The Packers were the most soft-bitten team in the league: they over-
whelmed one, underwhelmed ten, and whelmed one."

DAVE MCNALLY
Baltimore Orioles pitcher, to teammate Brooks Robinson after Robinson
made three errors in the first eight games of the 1974 season:

"You've gone from a human vacuum cleaner to a litterbug."

ROGER KAHN
writer:

"For the Washington Senators, the worst time of the year is the baseball season."

LEE TREVINO
professional golfer, on fellow tour player J. C. Snead:

"He was so ugly as a kid, his parents tied pork chops around his neck so that the dog would play with him."

CONNIE STEVENS
actress, on Joe Namath:

"Who wants to go with a guy who's got two bad knees and a quick release?"

RAY GANDOLF
sportscaster, on Muhammad Ali at age 39:

"He floats like an anchor, stings like a moth."

TOMMY LASORDA
Los Angeles Dodgers manager:

"When Billy Martin reaches for a bar tab, his arm shrinks six inches."

DICK OTTE
newspaper editor, on Woody Hayes:

"Woody grew up to be the man his father told him not to associate with."

MUHAMMAD ALI
heavyweight boxing champion, on Howard Cosell:

"Sometimes I wish I was a dog and he was a fire hydrant."

JIMMY CANNON
sportswriter:

"If Howard Cosell were a sport, he'd be roller derby."

AL MCGUIRE
sportscaster and former Marquette basketball coach, asked what sort of basketball player former broadcasting partner Billy Packer was at Wake Forest:

"He had a great outside shot, but he forgot that basketball is played indoors."

TIM MCCARVER
Philadelphia Phillies catcher, formerly of St. Louis:

"I remember one time going out on the mound to talk with Bob Gibson. He told me to get back behind the batter, that the only thing I knew about pitching was it was hard to hit."

(Dave McNally, Baltimore Orioles pitching coach, on manager Earl Weaver: "The only thing Earl knows about pitching is that he couldn't hit it.")

ARCHIE GRIFFIN
former Ohio State running back, on coach Woody Hayes:

"He doesn't know anything about drugs. He still thinks uppers are dentures."

LOU HOLTZ
Arkansas football coach, on slow-footed quarterback Kevin Scanlon:

"When he runs the ball we use a lot more film."

GRANTLAND RICE
New York sportswriter, responding before a dinner audience to Illinois coach Bob Zuppke's characterization of New York sportswriting as "the cesspool of journalism":

"My friend Zup's remarks on New York journalism remind me of the advice my old grandmother gave me before I left Tennessee. 'Grantland,' she said, 'never get into an argument about cesspools with a man who is an expert.' "

ROONE ARLEDGE
ABC Sports president, after Howard Cosell's debut as a football commentator:

"Howard, we are not paying you by the syllable."

CATFISH HUNTER
New York Yankees pitcher, asked if he ever tasted one of Reggie Jackson's Reggie Bars:

"I unwrapped it and it told me how good it was."

PEPPER MARTIN
former St. Louis Cardinals third baseman/outfielder, responding to former Cardinals executive Branch Rickey at a reunion of the 1934 team after Rickey praised the players as men who loved the game so much they would have played for nothing:

"Thanks to you, Mr. Rickey, we almost did."

BOB HOPE
comedian, on former U.S. President Gerald Ford:

"We have 51 golf courses in Palm Springs. He never decides which course he will play until after his first tee shot."

DAN QUISENBERRY
Kansas City Royals pitcher, on the control problems of teammate Renie Martin:

"Some people throw to spots, some people throw to zones. Renie throws to continents."

BOBBY BOWDEN
Florida State football coach, on linebacker Reggie Herring:

"He doesn't know the meaning of the word fear. In fact, I just saw his grades, and he doesn't know the meaning of a lot of words."

WILLIE STARGELL
Pittsburgh Pirates outfielder, told that teammate Dave Parker had called Stargell his idol:

"That's pretty good, considering that Dave's previous idol was himself."

Recruits and Recruiting

ANONYMOUS

"Recruiting is like shaving. Do it every day or you will look like a bum."

LOU HOLTZ
Arkansas football coach:

"What I'm looking for is a running back who can carry the ball 20 times on Saturday and then show up at practice Monday without a lawyer, doctor or agent."

THEODORE MCKELDIN
Maryland governor, in response to Queen Elizabeth when she inquired, prior to the 1957 Maryland–North Carolina football game, "Where do you get all those enormous players?":

"Your Majesty, that's a very embarrassing question."

GEORGE REVELING
Washington State basketball coach:

"When the athletic director said I should recruit more white players to keep the folks in Pullman happy, I signed Rufus White and Willie White."

LOU HOLTZ
Arkansas football coach, on why he almost didn't recruit a defensive lineman who looked weak:

"If we won a game, I didn't know if he would be strong enough to carry me off the field."

ALEX AGASE
Purdue football coach, asked why he avoids recruiting in California:

"Any kid who would leave that wonderful weather is too dumb to play for us."

ABE LEMONS
Texas basketball coach, on press brochures:

"Just once I'd like to see a picture of one of these guys with the caption 'He's a dog' underneath it. 'Ate up $8,000 worth of groceries in four years and can't play worth a lick.' "

TONY MASON

Arizona football coach, comparing his recruiting with that of John Robinson at the University of Southern California:

"I sell cactus; he sells Heismans."

GEORGE REVELING

Washington State basketball coach:

"The position of UCLA and USC in athletics is like the Arabs in oil. By a quirk of nature they're sitting on 50 percent of the world's supply."

LOU HOLTZ

Arkansas football coach:

"The guys I want to talk to are the guys who ride motorcycles on the [Southern California] freeways. Talk about courage."

BERNIE BIERMAN

former Minnesota football coach, recalling his recruiting technique:

"I would stop and ask directions to the nearest town, and if the farm boy would merely point, I'd go on my way. But if he held up his plow and pointed, I'd sign him on the spot."
   (Doc Spears, a Bierman predecessor at the Minnesota football helm, was fond of telling a similar story about his recruitment of legendary tackle and fullback Bronko Nagurski.)

DUFFY DAUGHERTY

Michigan State football coach, on the type of player he prefers:

"We like them big at Michigan State. But we'll settle for players with three kinds of bones—a funny bone, a wishbone and a backbone. The funny bone is to enjoy a laugh, even at one's own expense. The wishbone is to think big, set one's goals high and to have dreams and ambitions. And the backbone—well, that's what a boy needs to get up and go to work and make all those dreams come true."

TOMMY VARDEMAN

Centenary College assistant basketball coach:

"Every team needs huggers. Those are the guys you sign so you can hug 'em after you win, instead of having to hug the guys who play and sweat."

ED MURPHY

New Mexico State assistant basketball coach, on recruiting high school players in the early seventies:

"Twenty years ago, all you had to do was tell a mother how good her pecan pie was, and you got her seven-foot son and a pie a month for four years. Now you take Mom and Dad to the Waldorf, where they order lobster because they have already tried everything else on the menu with sixteen other coaches."

208

JOHNNY JOHNSON
Texas assistant football coach:

"Recruiting against USC is like trying to fight a tank with a baseball bat."

LAKE KELLY
onetime Oral Roberts basketball coach, on the problem with coaching at the Tulsa school:

"If you're going to the Final Four, you have to recruit athletes, not Christians."

ABE LEMONS
Oklahoma City basketball coach, offering a solution to recruiting excesses:

"Just give every coach the same amount of money and tell him he can keep what's left over."

KNUTE ROCKNE
Notre Dame football coach, decrying recruiting in 1929:

"I think it would be a wonderful thing if a coach could just forget all about the high school and prep school wonders of the world and develop a team from among the students of his institution who came to his school because they liked it best and not because of any attractive offers made for athletic ability."

Retirement

GEORGE HALAS
Chicago Bears owner:

"I knew it was time to quit [coaching] when I was chewing out an official and he walked off the penalty faster than I could keep up with him."

JOHN FITZGERALD
Dallas Cowboys center, explaining why he decided to continue his career despite having called a press conference to announce his retirement:

"When nobody showed up, I said the heck with it and decided to play another year."

MICKEY HERSKOWITZ
sportscaster:

"Since they are using newsmen as a negotiating tactic, every athlete announcing his retirement should be required to post a bond. If he comes out of retirement within 60 days, he forfeits the bond and distributes the sum equally among writers attending his original press conference."

EARLY WYNN
American League pitcher still active at age 40, asked about his retirement plans:

"Somebody will have to come out and take the uniform off me, and the guy who comes after it better bring help."

ROD THORN
Chicago Bulls general manager:

"Players think they're going to be around forever. But forever has a way of coming a lot sooner than they think."

RED BLAIK
former Army football coach, asked if he missed the game in retirement:

"I did at first, but after a while—well, you can't imagine how it feels not to have to sit still and watch an 18-year-old kid run out on that field with your salary check fluttering between his fingers."

ED DOHERTY
Arizona football coach, asked what he planned to do upon retirement:

"I'm going to tuck a football under my arm and head south of the border. When I get far enough south for someone to ask, 'What's that thing you're carrying?' that's where I'm going to settle down."

SANDY KOUFAX
Los Angeles Dodgers pitcher, asked why he was allowing elbow arthritis to force his retirement while he was in his prime:

"When I'm 40 years old, I'd still like to be able to comb my hair."

STEVE HOVLEY
Oakland A's outfielder:

"They're going to retire my uniform—with me still in it."

Rookies

PETER GENT
Dallas Cowboys receiver, advising a
rookie about coach Tom Landry's
huge playbook:

"Don't bother reading it, kid.
Everybody gets killed in the
end."

COTTON FITZSIMMONS
NBA coach:

"I wait until I see a rookie doing a shaving commercial on TV.
Then I figure he might be ready to play."

BILL FITCH
Boston Celtics coach:

"Ask a rookie the difference between the regular season and the
playoffs and he'll tell you it's that he didn't play in the playoffs."

MARV LEVY
professional football coach:

"People expect too much from rookies; rookies don't expect
enough of themselves."

Rules

ANONYMOUS

"All may be fair in love and war, but in sport nothing is fair but the rules."

HERBERT HOOVER
thirty-first president of the United States:

"The rigid volunteer rules of right and wrong in sports are second only to religious faith in moral training."

ABE LEMONS
Texas basketball coach:

"If I make a set of rules, then a guy goes out and steals an airplane. He comes back and says, 'It wasn't on the list of rules.' "

TOMMY MASON
Cincinnati University football coach:

"The thing about colleges abiding by the rules is that 90 percent of them do it, and the other 10 percent go to the bowl games."

BILL VEECK
major league baseball owner:

"I try not to break the rules but merely to test their elasticity."

BUZZIE BAVASI
major league baseball executive:

"We live by the Golden Rule. Those who have the gold make the rules."

JACK KELLY
AAU president, on rules governing amateur sport:

"If every illegal sex act were policed properly, 75 percent of the population would have been in jail. The same goes for

CARL MAUCK
Houston Oilers center, after being fined $250 by NFL Commissioner Pete Rozelle for allowing his shirttail to hang out during a nationally televised game:

"In the off-season NFL players rob banks, forge checks and sell dope to kids, and Rozelle does nothing. Then he fines me for a shirttail."

VINCE LOMBARDI
Green Bay Packers coach, upon fining receiver Max McGee $500 for breaking curfew a second time, twice what he had fined him for his first offense:

"And the next time it'll be $1,000. And if you find anything worth $1,000, let me know and I may go with you."

amateur athletics. There are few world-class amateurs left in any sport."

ABE LEMONS
Oklahoma City basketball coach:

"When you have a curfew, it's always your star who gets caught."

Schedules

ABE LEMONS
Texas basketball coach:

"Coaches who shoot par in the summer are the guys I want on my schedule in the winter."

CAL STOLLE
Minnesota University football coach:

"We finally got Nebraska where we want them—off the schedule."

JOE PATERNO
Penn State football coach, asked when Alabama and Notre Dame would appear on the Nittany Lions' schedule:

"The year after I retire."

ABE LEMONS
Texas basketball coach:

"I'll give a lecture in a clinic and look for the guy who's taking notes. That's the guy I want to schedule a game with next year."

Self-Disparagement

BUM PHILLIPS
Houston Oilers coach, asked whether he played college football:

"I thought I did until I looked at some old game films."

MILLER BARBER
professional golfer:

"I don't say my golf game is bad, but if I grew tomatoes they'd come up sliced."

BOB UECKER
baseball broadcaster and former major leaguer:

"Anybody with ability can play in the big leagues. But to be able to trick people year in and year out the way I did, I think that's a much greater feat."

LEFTY GOMEZ
Hall of Fame pitcher:

"I had most of my trouble with left-handed hitters. Charley Gehringer could hit me in a tunnel at midnight with the lights out."

JOHN MCKAY
Tampa Buccaneers coach:

"I don't know a thing about kicking except it takes tempo like a golf swing. And if you've ever seen me play golf, you know I don't know a thing about tempo."

DON SUTTON
Los Angeles Dodgers pitcher, on Houston Astros pitcher J. R. Richard at the height of Richard's success:

"I'm sick of hearing about J. Rodney Richard. We all know what he can do with his stuff. He's tremendous. But what I'd like to see is what he could do with *my* stuff."

BEAR BRYANT
Alabama football coach:

"I ain't won but one. My team won the rest in spite of me."

BOB HOPE
comedian, on his schoolboy football days:

"I was known as Neckline Hope. I was always plunging down the middle but never really showing anything."

TEX SCHRAMM
Dallas Cowboys president, after holdout running back Duane Thomas called him "sick and demented" and "dishonest":

"That's not bad. He got two out of three."

CASEY STENGEL
New York Yankees manager, testifying before a senate subcommittee evaluating legislation to exempt baseball from federal antitrust laws:

"I had many years that I was not so successful as a ballplayer, as it is a game of skill."

TONY MARTIN
singer, recalling his brief baseball career:

"The report on me was that I was a switch hitter who struck out both ways, but I could sing for the team on the bus."

BARNEY SCHULTZ
St. Louis Cardinals pitcher, explaining why he called one of his deliveries the "mattress pitch" during the 1964 World Series:

"I threw it and the Yankees laid on it."

CASEY STENGEL
New York Yankees manager, on his major league debut as a player with the Brooklyn Dodgers:

"I broke in with four hits, and the writers promptly decided they had seen the new Ty Cobb. It took me only a few days to correct that assumption."

HAYDEN FRY
Southern Methodist University football coach:

"I'm the oratorical equivalent of a blocked punt."

TIP O'NEILL
Speaker of the House, on playing Maryland's famed Congressional Country Club course:

"If I swing the gavel the way I swing a golf club, no wonder the nation's in a hell of a mess."

LEE TREVINO
professional golfer, comparing his drives with those of Jack Nicklaus:

"If he'd had to play my tee ball all his life, he'd be a pharmacist."

WILMER "VINEGAR BEN" MIZELL
North Carolina congressman and former major league pitcher:

"I'm anxious to see some of the moon-rock samples the astronauts brought back. I'm sure there are a few of my home-run balls in that crowd."

LYNDON B. JOHNSON,
thirty-sixth President of the United States:

"I don't have any handicap. I am all handicap."

Sex

CASEY STENGEL
major league manager:

"You gotta learn that if you don't get it by midnight, chances are you ain't gonna get it; and if you do, it ain't worth it."

BRUCE JENNER
Olympic decathlon champion:

"The only time sex has bothered me is when I do it during the competition."

CASEY STENGEL
major league manager:

"Being with a woman all night never hurt no professional baseball player. It's staying up all night looking for a woman that does him in."

SEVERIANO BALLESTEROS
professional golfer, asked if he was committed to one woman:

"No, that would be like playing the same golf course all the time."

Showmanship

LEE TREVINO
professional golfer:

"You've got to back it up with your sticks. I played the tour in 1967 and told jokes and nobody laughed. Then I won the Open the next year, told the same jokes and everybody laughed like hell."

WILLIE MAYS
Hall of Fame center fielder:

"When I was 17 years old I realized I was in a form of show business. It's like being an actor on the Broadway stage. He doesn't phrase his part exactly the same way every day. He thinks up new things. So I played for the fans, and I wanted to make sure each fan that came out would see something different I did each day."

WALTER HAGEN
professional golfer:

"Make the hard ones look easy and the easy ones look hard."

BOB THOMAS
Chicago Bears placekicker, explaining why he prefers to have his field-goal attempts hit the crossbar before clearing it:

"When I kick them through the uprights, I never get on the 10 o'clock news."

BILL VEECK
major league baseball owner:

"People identify with the swashbuckling individuals, not polite little men who field their positions well. Sir Galahad had a big following, but I'll bet Lancelot had more."

JACK RENNER
professional golfer:

"How do you be funny when you have a six-foot putt for $54,-000?"

Skiing

ERMA BOMBECK
humorist:

"I do not participate in any sport with ambulances at the bottom of a hill."

JOHN F. KENNEDY
1960 U.S. presidential candidate, asked why he was abstaining from the sport during the campaign:

"My own profession is hazardous enough."

Soccer

PHIL WOOSNAM
North American Soccer League commissioner:

"The rules are very simple. Basically it's this: If it moves, kick it; if it doesn't move, kick it until it does."

RINUS MICHELS
Los Angeles Aztecs coach, asked how many years it would take the U.S. to produce a great soccer player:

"Five. That's how long it takes for naturalization, isn't it?"

ELIZABETH TAYLOR
actress:

"I prefer rugby to soccer. When soccer players start biting each other's ears off again, maybe I'll like it better."

PAUL CANNELL
Washington Diplomats player, explaining why he dropped his shorts during an NASL game:

"I was trying to give the league a little exposure."

Sport

ROONE ARLEDGE
ABC Sports president:

"Sport is a set of created circumstances—artificial circumstances—set up to frustrate a man in pursuit of a goal. He has to have certain skills to overcome those obstacles—or even to challenge them. And people who don't have those skills cheer him and admire him."

FRANKLIN ROOSEVELT
thirty-second President of the United States:

"Sport is the very fiber of all we stand for. It keeps our spirits alive."

DAVID RIESMAN
sociologist:

"The road to the boardroom leads through the locker room."

WILFRID SHEED
writer:

"Sports constitute a code, a language of emotions—and a tourist who skips the stadiums will not recoup his losses at Lincoln Center and Grant's Tomb."

BOB WOOLF
agent, on sports in the seventies:

"These days it's not as important to know the difference between a veer offense and a wishbone as to know the difference between a preliminary hearing and a temporary injunction."

NEIL SIMON
playwright/screenwriter:

"Sports is the only entertainment where, no matter how many times you go back, you never know the ending."

TED TURNER
Atlanta Braves and Hawks owner:

"Sports is like a war without the killing."

JIMMY CANNON
sportswriter:

"Sports is the toy department of life."

JAMES CAAN
actor:

"If you watch a drama, after five minutes you know the guy's going to get the girl or not get the girl, or whatever. In sports, the end is unknown. Sports is life itself, and that's why I never get tired of it."

KEITH JACKSON
sportscaster:

"Sports, more than any other activity, has proven that a truly democratic society owes the individual nothing more than opportunity."

JEAN-PAUL SARTRE
French philosopher:

"Play is an activity . . . for which man himself sets the rules, and which has no consequences except according to the rules posited."

IRVIN S. COBB
humorist:

"As I understand it, sport is hard work for which you do not get paid."

BENJAMIN FRANKLIN
statesman/scientist/philosopher:

"Games lubricate the body and the mind."

ROY HOFHEINZ
Houston Astros owner, after building the $37 million Astrodome:

"I've got a ten-thousand-dollar-a-day overhead here, and to treat sport like sport is to fail to understand the seriousness of your business."

WELLS TWOMBLY
sportswriter, in 1972:

"Anybody who has lived through the incomparable greed of the past ten years and still thinks that sweating in public still has its uplifting aspects needs ten hours with a good shrink."

ANDREW MULLIGAN
English writer:

"Sport is an exportable commodity, like language and cuisine."

H. L. MENCKEN
essayist and editor:

"I hate all sports as rabidly as a person who likes sports hates common sense."

DON NIELSEN
1980 U. S. Olympic biathlon team member, describing his sport:

"It's like smoking a pack of cigarettes, then running a 440-yard dash, and then trying to thread a needle."

DOUGLAS MACARTHUR
U.S. Army five-star general:

Upon the fields of friendly strife
Are sown the seeds,
That, upon other fields, on other days,
Will bear the fruits of victory.

GEORGE BERNARD SHAW
British playwright/novelist:

"It is a noteworthy fact that kicking and beating have played so considerable a part in the habits of which necessity has imposed on mankind in past ages that the only way of preventing civilized men from kicking and beating their wives is to organize games in which they can kick and beat balls."

PAUL GARDNER
English writer:

"It has often occurred to me that sport, like sex, is an activity that should be either performed or watched—but not written about."

FRANK HOWARD
Clemson athletic director, refusing to incorporate crew into the school's athletic program:

"We ain't gonna have no sport where you sit down and go backwards."

WILLIAM SHAKESPEARE
British dramatist/poet:

If all the year were playing holidays,
To sport would be as tedious as to work.

JIM MURRAY
sportswriter:

"The only thing I know for sure about sports is that they need dramatizing."

226

Sport Comparisons

KEN HARRELSON
former major league baseball player attempting a switch to professional golf:

"In baseball you hit a home run over the right-field fence, the left-field fence, the center-field fence. Nobody cares. In golf, everything has got to be right over second base."

EARL WEAVER
Baltimore Orioles manager, on why he prefers baseball to football:

"You can't sit on a lead and run a few plays into the line and just kill the clock. You've got to throw the ball over the goddamn plate and give the other man a chance."

DON CARTER
professional bowler:

"One of the advantages of bowling over golf is that you very seldom lose a bowling ball."

HOWARD COSELL
sportscaster:

"In general, I find boxers possess more wisdom than baseball players. In baseball, the principal level of conversation is last night's sexual conquest."

AL FARMER
rodeo performer-turned-race driver:

"When you get a car on top of you, you just lie there and somebody comes to pick you up; but you get a bull on top of you and you've still gotta outrun the bull to the fence."

LES LEAR
horse trainer, comparing his vocation with football coaching:

"All I can say is you know where the horses are at night."

GEORGE RAVELING
Washington State basketball coach, revealing how he first became involved in the game:

"When I went to a Catholic high school in Philadelphia, we just had one coach for football and basketball. He took all of us who turned out and had us run through a forest. The ones who ran into the trees went on the football team."

GEORGE PLIMPTON
writer, hypothesizing that there is an inverse correlation between the size of a ball and the quality of writing about the sport in which the ball is used:

"There are superb books about golf, very good books about baseball, not many good books about football and very few good books about basketball. There are no books about beach balls."

Y. A. TITTLE
New York Giants quarterback, on why a baseball pitcher like Warren Spahn is more durable than a pro football quarterback:

"Spahn throws a baseball and some other guy hits it with a bat. I throw a football, and right after that a lot of guys weighing 250 pounds hit me."

BILL RODGERS
marathon runner:

"Passing a football straight is nice and dandy, but I think it's an inferior skill. I'll be running over Joe Namath's grave."

EMLEN TUNNELL
New York Giants safety:

"Tackling is football. Running is track."

SAM SNEAD
professional golfer, on why his sport is more challenging than baseball:

"In golf, when we hit a foul ball, we got to go out and play it."

ROGERS HORNSBY
Hall of Fame infielder, expressing his preference for baseball over golf:

"When I hit a ball I want someone else to go chase it."

VIN SCULLY
sportscaster:

"Football is to baseball as blackjack is to bridge. One is the quick jolt; the other the deliberate, slow-paced game of skill."

BRAD DILLMAN
actor, explaining his preference for golf over tennis:

"All tennis courts look alike."

LEO NOMELLINI
San Francisco 49ers lineman who later became a professional wrestler, on which sport is more demanding:

"Oh, wrestling is much tougher. Every night you have to drive a lot of miles to another arena."

ROGER KAHN
writer:

"Football is violence and cold weather and sex and college rye. Horse racing is animated roulette. Boxing is smoky halls and kidneys battered until they bleed. Tennis and golf are best played, not watched. Basketball, hockey, and track meets are action heaped upon action, climax

---

JOHN MCKAY
Tampa Bay Buccaneers coach, comparing college and pro football:

"Both games are great. The colleges have all the leaves turning brown, and we've got the girls with the big chests."

upon climax, until the onlooker's responses become deadened. Baseball is for the leisurely afternoons of summer and for the unchanging dreams."

JOHN LEONARD
writer:

"Baseball happens to be a game of cumulative tension. . . . Football, basketball and hockey are played with hand grenades and machine guns."

HENRY BLAHA
Baltimore Rugby Club captain:

"They say that rugby is a beastly game played by gentlemen, that soccer is a gentlemen's game played by beasts, and that football is a beastly game played by beasts."

SAM SNEAD
professional golfer:

"I shot a wild elephant in Africa 30 yards from me, and it didn't hit the ground until it was right at my feet. I wasn't a bit scared. But a 4-foot putt scares me to death."

TED SOLOTAROFF
writer/editor:

"A professional football team warms up grimly and disparately, like an army on maneuvers: the ground troops here, the tanks there, the artillery and air force over there. Basketball teams, after the perfunctory lay-up drill, fall into the crowded isolation and personal style of ten city kids shooting at the same basket or playing one-on-one. A baseball team horses around the batting cage, leisurely shags flies, romps across the outfield, chats with the other team; the atmosphere is as frisky and relaxed as a county fair."

GEORGE BERNARD SHAW
British playwright/novelist:

"Baseball has the great advantage over cricket of being sooner ended."

STEVE SMITH
pole-vaulter:

"I never did like team sports because of the coaches. In individual sports they coach you to develop specific skills. But in team sports they just yell at you. If I wanted somebody to yell at me, I'd join the Army."

TOM PACIOREK
Chicago White Sox first baseman and onetime linebacker at Houston University:

"The only reason I played baseball at all in college was to get out of spring football."

VIC SPELLBERG
powerboat racer:

"Offshore racing is like jumping into a cold shower, taking a baseball bat and hitting yourself over the head with it—while at the same time you're tearing up $100 bills as fast as you can."

HENRY AARON
Hall of Fame outfielder:

"It took me 17 years to get 3,000 hits in baseball. I did it in one afternoon on the golf course."

Sportsmanship

MARK TWAIN
writer:

"It's good sportsmanship to not pick up lost golf balls while they are still rolling."

PAT CULPEPPER
Texas linebacker, accepting the Swede Nelson sportsmanship award:

"I've been thinking a lot about sportsmanship. It's hard to define—especially in football, which starts with premeditated mayhem."

ALISTAIR COOKE
English newsman/historian:

"Sport and sportsmanship have the same root, but sportsmen are a disappearing species."

KNUTE ROCKNE
Notre Dame football coach:

"One man practicing sportsmanship is far better than a hundred teaching it."

Sportswriters

RED SMITH
sportswriter:

"Writing a column is like opening a vein and letting the words bleed out, drip by drip."

FRANK BOGGS
sports editor:

"During my career I have covered four professional teams on a full-time basis—the Dallas Cowboys, the San Diego Chargers, the Denver Broncos and the University of Oklahoma Sooners."

GEORGE RAVELING
Washington State basketball coach:

"The best three years of a sportswriter's life are the third grade."

BOBBY KNIGHT
Indiana basketball coach:

"All of us learn to write by the second grade, then most of us go on to other things."

CLIFF TEMPLE
English sportswriter:

"A [sports] journalist is someone who would if he could but he can't, so he tells those who already can how they should."

JIMMY CANNON
sportswriter:

"A sportswriter is entombed in a prolonged boyhood."

JOE PATERNO
Penn State football coach:

"If I ever need a brain transplant, I want one from a sportswriter, because I'll know it's never been used."

BOBBY KNIGHT
Indiana basketball coach:

"Absolute silence—that's the one thing a sportswriter can quote accurately."

SAM SNEAD
professional golfer:

"I once thought of becoming a political cartoonist because they only have to come up with one idea a day. Then I thought I'd become a sportswriter instead, because they don't have to come up with any."

RED SMITH
sportswriter:

"Any sportswriter who thinks the world is no bigger than the outfield fence is not only a bad citizen of the world but also a lousy sportswriter."

HAROLD BALLARD
Toronto Maple Leafs owner, on women in the locker room:

"If they want to take their clothes off and talk to the players, fine. But I warn them, they'll have a lot more trouble getting out than they did getting in."

RICHARD M. NIXON
thirty-seventh President of the United States:

"If I had my life to live over, I would have liked to have ended up as a sportswriter."

STANLEY WOODWARD
sportswriter, in his first column for the New York *Herald-Tribune* since being fired 11 years earlier:

"As I was saying when I was so rudely interrupted 11 years ago . . ."

WOODY PAIGE
sportswriter, in response to a woman in a hotel bar who told him she would do anything he wanted for $100:

"I'm in Room 123. Go up and write a column and a sidebar."

RED SMITH
sportswriter, asked his plans after editors of *The New York Times* killed a column in which he advocated a boycott of the 1980 Moscow Olympics in protest over the Soviets' military presence in Afghanistan:

"I'll write about the infield fly rule."

Stadiums

JOE ROBBIE
Miami Dolphins owner, on the city's offer to spend $2.5 million to refurbish the Orange Bowl:

"Spending money on that place would be like taking a button and sewing a new suit around it."

LINDSEY NELSON
sportscaster, recalling the Dodgers' first home in Los Angeles:

"They had room at the Los Angeles Coliseum for 93,000 people and two outfielders."

ART LINKLETTER
TV personality, anticipating the Dodgers' 1958 debut in the spacious Los Angeles Memorial Coliseum:

"My tickets in the Coliseum are seat 67, aisle 72, Highway 99."

BUD ADAMS
Houston Oilers owner:

"If the Astrodome is the eighth wonder of the world, the rent is the ninth."

JOHN UPDIKE
writer:

"Fenway Park, in Boston, is a lyric little bandbox of a ball park. Everything is painted green and seems in curiously sharp focus, like the inside of an old-fashioned peeping-type Easter egg."

GABE PAUL
Cleveland Indians president, on the Houston Astrodome:

"It will revolutionize baseball. It will open a new area of alibis for the players."

STAN MUSIAL
St. Louis Cardinals first baseman, on the advent of domed stadiums:

"I got started too early in baseball. In air conditioning I could have lasted 20 years longer."

RAY WALSTON
actor, on the Houston Astrodome:

"It shows what you can get if you really look through the Neiman-Marcus catalog."

JOHN F. DUNN
Illinois congressman, arguing that the Chicago Cubs should be permitted to install lights in their stadium despite the concerns of area residents:

"Noise pollution at Wrigley Field can't be that much of a problem. There's nothing there to cheer about."

GEORGE GAINFORD
fight manager:

"It ain't the number of seats you got, it's the number of asses that are in 'em."

Statistics

JIM BOUTON
major league pitcher:

"Statistics are about as interesting as first-base coaches."

BOBBY BRAGAN
Milwaukee Braves manager, on baseball people's reliance on statistics:

"Say you were standing with one foot in the oven and one foot in an ice bucket. According to the percentage people, you should be perfectly comfortable."

ROGER M. BLOUGH
U.S. Steel chairman, on his football-playing days at Susquehanna University:

"In the three years I played, we won six, lost 17 and tied two. Some statistician with a great capacity for charity has calculated that we won 75 percent of the games we didn't lose."

TOBY HARRAH
Cleveland Indians third baseman, claiming that baseball statistics are like a girl in a bikini:

"They both show a lot, but not everything."

Success

JOHN WOODEN
UCLA basketball coach:

"Success is peace of mind which is a direct result of self-satisfaction in knowing you did your best to become the best that you are capable of becoming."

EDWARD KENNEDY
U.S. senator:

"I don't think you're going to be a success in anything if you think about losing, whether it's in sports or in politics."

LEFTY GOMEZ
Hall of Fame pitcher:

"The secret of my success was clean living and a fast-moving outfield."

CHARLIE FINLEY
Oakland A's owner:

"Sweat plus sacrifice equals success."

EDDIE ARCARO
jockey:

"Once a guy starts wearing silk pajamas, it's hard to get up early."

VIC BRADEN
tennis instructor:

"The moment of enlightenment is when a person's dreams of possibilities become images of probabilities."

RANDY "TEX" COBB
heavyweight boxer:

"People always ask me if success is going to change me, and I tell them I sure hope so."

Superstars

CHARLIE WATERS
Dallas Cowboys safety, after watching a computerized game involving a mythical team of all-time greats including Jim Thorpe:

"For an 84-year-old Indian, he showed me some moves."

LOU HOLTZ
Arkansas football coach:

"Great players come and great players go. The graveyards are full of indispensable people."

WILLIE MAYS
Hall of Fame outfielder:

"It isn't hard to be good from time to time in sports. What's tough is being good every day."

JIM GILLIAM
Los Angeles Dodgers coach:

"There are some great ballplayers, but there aren't any superstars. Superstars you find on the moon."

WILLIE MCCOVEY
San Francisco Giants first baseman in 1978:

"I don't think baseball has a superstar today, regardless of what the salaries say. Henry Aaron, Willie Mays, Joe DiMaggio were superstars."

BOB ZUPPKE
Illinois football coach:

"My definition of an All-American is a player who has weak opposition and a poet in the press box."

Superstition

DUFFY DAUGHERTY
Michigan State football coach:

"My only feeling about superstition is that it's unlucky to be behind at the end of a game."
   (Also attributed to Bill Russell, Boston Celtics coach)

BABE RUTH
Hall of Fame outfielder:

"I have only one superstition. I make sure to touch all the bases when I hit a home run."

GEORGE UNDERWOOD
East Tennessee State forward, asked if he had any superstitions:

"Yes, two. One, don't call someone a bad name if they have a loaded pistol. Two, don't call your girl friend Tina if her name is Vivien."

JOHN CAMPANA
Bucknell offensive lineman:

"I don't like to jump from tall buildings before big games."

PHIL ESPOSITO
professional hockey player:

"I have these all over my locker area: four-leaf clover, Jewish star, Chinese good-luck charm. I can't afford to offend anyone."

GEORGE ARCHER
professional golfer:

"I don't like number 4 balls. And I don't like fives, sixes or sevens on my cards."

Surgery

BILL WALTON
San Diego Clippers center:

"I learned a long time ago that minor surgery is when they do the operation on someone else, not you."

LEFTY GOMEZ
Hall of Fame pitcher, after undergoing a heart bypass operation years after his retirement from baseball:

"If I'd known the operation was going to be that easy, I'd have had it when I was five years old."

TOMMY JOHN
New York Yankees pitcher, recalling his 1974 arm surgery:

"When they operated, I told them to put in a Koufax fastball. They did—but it was a *Mrs.* Koufax fastball."

DON CRIQUI
sportscaster:

"Lee Trevino doesn't want to talk about his back operation. That's all behind him."

E. J. HOLUB
former Kansas City Chiefs linebacker, on his 12 knee operations:

"My knees look like they lost a knife fight with a midget."

Tennis

BILLIE JEAN KING
professional tennis player, characterizing her sport:

"A perfect combination of violent action taking place in an atmosphere of total tranquility."

VIC BRADEN
tennis instructor:

"Losers have tons of variety. Champions take pride in just learning to hit the same old boring winners."

JOE JARES
sportswriter, on the lack of American success at the U.S. Open in the late fifties and early sixties:

"Alien lands provide the finalists, and the U.S. provides the ball boys."

BILL TILDEN
amateur champion, on how to play effective mixed doubles:

"Hit at the girl whenever possible."

BUD COLLINS
TV commentator:

"My uncle always describes an unforced error as his first marriage."

VIC BRADEN
tennis instructor, claiming tennis is an easy game:

"My theory is that if you buy an ice-cream cone and make it hit your mouth, you can play. If you stick it on your forehead, your chances are less."

Tough Guys

GUTHRIE PACKHARD
Denver Stars (major league rodeo)
owner, on the toughness of bars in the
area:

"I know a bar out on East
Colfax that's so tough, if you
don't have a gun when you go
in, they give you one."

JOHN WAYNE
actor, on why he quit bowling:

"There weren't many alleys
that would let me come back. I
have an overhand delivery."

MAURICE LUCAS
New York Knicks forward:

"I'm a blue-collar worker. I don't punch in, I punch out."

BIG DADDY LIPSCOMB,
NFL defensive tackle, on his tackling technique:

"I just wrap my arms around the whole backfield and peel 'em
off one by one until I get to the ball carrier. Him I keep."

DICK BUTKUS
Chicago Bears linebacker:

"I wouldn't ever set out to hurt anybody deliberately unless it
was, you know, important—like a league game or something."

MONTE CLARK
Detroit Lions coach, on running back Larry Csonka:

"When he goes on a safari, the lions roll up their windows."

JACK TATUM
Oakland Raiders defensive back:

"I never make a tackle just to bring someone down. I want to
punish the man I'm going after, and I want him to know that
it's going to hurt every time he comes my way."

DAVID HANNAH
Alabama tackle, denying stories that he and his NFL-playing brothers John and
Charles used to go after each other with two-by-fours:

"Naw, that's not so. It was with baseball bats."

DOUG PLANK
Chicago Bears defensive back, on former Bears linebacker Dick Butkus:

"Butkus was unbelievable. I love to see—and listen—to him
play. On the sound track of the Bears films, Butkus—when he's
going after somebody—sounds like a lion chewing on a big hunk
of meat."

MIKE DITKA
Dallas Cowboys tight end, on his reputation for meanness:

"I'm not mean at all. I just try to protect myself. And you'll see I don't ever pick on anybody who has a number above 30."

Track and Field

JONES RAMSAY
Texas University publicist:

"The only thing duller than track is field."

PAUL O'NEIL
writer:

"The art of running the mile consists, in essence, of reaching the
threshold of unconsciousness at the instant of breasting the
tape."

RICHARD ARMOUR
writer/poet:

> Track records would fall
> And last many a year
> If the chap with the torch
> Were to run from the rear.

MICHEL LOURIE
French sprint coach, asked why his country has been so much more successful
producing great wines than great track-and-field teams:

"Perhaps it is precisely because of our great wines that we have
not had great track teams."

Trades

BRANCH RICKEY
major league baseball executive:

"Trade a player a year too early rather than a year too late."

CLAUSE OSTEEN
Los Angeles Dodgers pitcher:

"I'm not sure which is more insulting, being offered in a trade or having it turned down."

BILL VEECK
Chicago White Sox owner, on his strategy of trading players frequently when he ran the old St. Louis Browns:

"I always felt the more Browns I could place on the other teams, the better off we would be."

JOE GARAGIOLA
sportscaster:

"Being traded is like celebrating your hundredth birthday. It might not be the happiest occasion in the world, but consider the alternatives."

BUM PHILLIPS
Houston Oilers coach:

"We're not giving away any football players who could hurt us later. I don't mind people thinking I'm stupid, but I don't want to give them any proof."

VERNON HOLLAND
Cincinnati Bengals tackle, recalling a dream in which he was traded:

"I don't know who got me. I dream in black and white, so I couldn't tell what color the suits were."

GRAIG NETTLES
New York Yankees third baseman, on pitcher Sparky Lyle after Lyle was traded to Texas following the 1978 season:

"He went from Cy Young to *sayonara* in a year."

PIERRE TRUDEAU
Canadian Prime Minister, on Canadian-American trade:

"Canada is a country whose main exports are hockey players and cold fronts. Our main imports are baseball players and acid rain."

CONRAD DOBLER
NFL defensive lineman, on his off-season trade from St. Louis to New Orleans:

"Religiously speaking, it is an advancement from a Cardinal to a Saint."

TOMMY MCVIE
Winnipeg Jets coach, bemoaning life in the NHL:

"Every time you try to make a deal with a general manager in this league, they give you snow in the winter; and if you're drowning, they throw you an anchor."

JOE GARAGIOLA
sportscaster and former major league baseball journeyman:

"I went through life as a 'player to be named later.'"

Verbosity

FRED AKERS
Texas football coach:

"Lou Holtz can talk faster than I can listen."

JOHN LARDNER
writer, on Casey Stengel:

"He can talk all day and all night, and on any kind of track, wet or dry."

CHICO RESCH
New York Islanders goalie:

"If I wasn't talking, I wouldn't know what to say."

BILL FITCH
Boston Celtics coach, on nonstop-talking guard B. B. Flenory:

"He may be the first player I've ever had who has to get his tonsils taped."

MARTY SPRINGSTEAD
American League umpire, on Baltimore Orioles manager Earl Weaver:

"The way to test a Timex watch would be to strap it to his tongue."

RING LARDNER
sportswriter, asked by Grantland Rice if he'd ever had a conversation with loquacious Michigan football coach Fielding Yost:

"No. My parents taught me never to interrupt."

JIM MURRAY
sports writer, upon the death of Casey Stengel:

"Well, God is certainly getting an earful tonight."

Violence

RODNEY DANGERFIELD
comedian:

"I went to a fight the other night, and a hockey game broke out."

CONN SMYTHE
Toronto Maple Leafs owner:

"We're going to have to do something about all this violence, or people are going to keep on buying tickets."

RON LYLE
heavyweight boxer:

"America wasn't built on going to church; it was built on violence. I express America in the ring."

IRWIN SHAW
writer, on football:

"If the players were armed with guns, there wouldn't be stadiums large enough to hold the crowds."

DR. ARNOLD BEISSER
psychiatrist:

"The old fan used to yell, 'Kill the umpire!' The new fan tries to do it."

Vocation Comparisons

TED TURNER
Atlanta Hawks and Braves owner, on the difference between being a baseball pitcher and a doctor:

"Make a wild pitch as a doctor and they bury you."

STEVE FULLER
Clemson quarterback, trying to decide between law and football for a profession:

"You either have to finesse 12 people who weren't smart enough to get out of jury duty, or 11 who weren't smart enough to play offense."

ED MARINARO
former Cornell running back who left a mediocre NFL career for acting:

"In football, if you're late for a workout they fine you. In acting, if you're late for a rehearsal they fire you."

EUGENE MCCARTHY
U.S. senator, on how politics is like coaching football:

"You have to be smart enough to understand the game and dumb enough to think it's important."

ABE LEMONS
Texas basketball coach, on why coaching is tougher than practicing medicine:

"Doctors bury their mistakes. We still have ours on scholarship."

ABE LEMONS
Texas basketball coach, complaining that coaches are put under inordinate scrutiny and pressure:

"Just once I'd like to see the win–loss records of doctors right out front where people could see them—won ten, lost three, tied two."

TED GIANNOULAS
the man who portrays the "San Diego Chicken" for fan entertainment at sporting events, asked if his mother didn't think his occupation was a bit foolish:

"Not at all. She thinks I'm a doctor in Wisconsin."

HARRY S. TRUMAN
thirty-third President of the United States:

"It's a lot tougher to be a football coach than a President. You've got four years as a President, and they guard you. A coach doesn't have anyone to protect him when things go wrong."

FRANK SINATRA
entertainer, admiring Bill Bradley:

"He's a basketball player and a U.S. senator. He's found the only two jobs I know where you only have to work a couple of hours a day."

TOMMY BELL
attorney and NFL official:

"During the week I practice law. On Sunday I *am* the law."

HOWARD COSELL
sportscaster:

"There are two professions that one can be hired at with little experience. One is prostitution. The other is sportscasting. Too frequently they become the same."

JACK KEMP
New York congressman and former NFL quarterback:

"In football, the enemy had numbers on and were out in front where you could see them. That's not always the case in politics."

Weather

ANONYMOUS HORSEPLAYER
complaining about the seeming perpetual chill at New York's Aqueduct racetrack:

"The four seasons here are early winter, winter, late winter and next winter."

TOMMY LASORDA
Los Angeles Dodgers manager, prior to the Dodgers' 1981 National League championship series with Montreal:

"The only way I'd worry about the weather is if it snows on our side of the field and not theirs."

CLAUDE HUMPHREY
Philadelphia Eagles defensive end, objecting to soaring temperatures at training camp in West Chester, Pennsylvania:

"If God wanted it so hot, why did He invent people?"

JOHN PAPANEK
sportswriter, recalling the weather he endured as an undergraduate at Michigan University:

"I remember one winter that was so bad I didn't go outside for three weeks. We used to send out for pizzas and use them for heat. When they cooled off, we ate them."

HERB CAEN
writer, on San Francisco's climate:

"We get baseball weather in football season and football weather in July and August."

TED GIANNOULAS
the man who portrays the "San Diego Chicken" for fan entertainment at sporting events, asked if his costume had been uncomfortable during a severe heat wave:

"If you can't stand the heat, stay out of The Chicken."

Winning and Losing

BILLY MARTIN
major league manager:

"When you're a professional, you come back no matter what happened the day before."

CLAUDE GILBERT
San Diego State football coach, after a 49-point loss to Brigham Young University:

"I feel kind of like the guy who lost playing Russian roulette. You know you're taking a chance; but by the time you hear the explosion, it's too late."

RED SANDERS
Vanderbilt football coach:

"Winning isn't everything, it's the only thing."
  (Invariably attributed, erroneously, to Vince Lombardi)

VINCE LOMBARDI
Green Bay Packers coach:

"Winning is not everything—but making the effort to win is."

AL MCGUIRE
Marquette basketball coach:

"Winning is overemphasized. The only time it is really important is in surgery and war."

JOHN R. TUNIS
writer:

"Losing is the great American sin."

DARRELL ROYAL
Texas football coach:

"The margin between victory and defeat is so small that you can't get too chesty when you win or too despondent when you lose."

GEORGE ALLEN
Washington Redskins coach:

"Every time you win, you're reborn; when you lose, you die a little."

BILLY MARTIN
major league manager:

"Everything looks nicer when you win. The girls are prettier. The cigars taste better. The trees are greener."

GEORGE S. KAUFMAN
playwright:

"I'd rather be a poor winner than any kind of loser."

CHRIS EVERT LLOYD
professional tennis player:

"It's tough being on top. It's lonely there. If you want to be the best, you can't be best friends with everybody."

BEAR BRYANT
Alabama football coach:

"They say I teach brutal football, but the only thing brutal about football is losing."

JOHN WOODEN
UCLA basketball coach:

"I don't know whether always winning is good. It breeds envy and distrust in others and overconfidence and a lack of appreciation very often in those who enjoy it."

VINCE LOMBARDI
NFL coach:

"If you can't accept losing, you can't win."

LEO DUROCHER
major league manager:

" 'How you play the game' is for college boys. When you're playing for money, winning is the only thing that counts."

GENE AUTRY
California Angels owner:

"Grantland Rice, the great sportswriter, once said, 'It's not whether you win or lose, it's how you play the game.' Well, Grantland Rice can go to hell as far as I'm concerned."

JAMES CAAN
actor:

"Someone's always saying, 'It's not whether you win or lose,' but if you feel that way, you're as good as dead."

DONALD DELL
tennis agent/commentator:

"I can't subscribe to that old cliché that it is not whether you win or lose, but how you play the game. In that case, why keep score?"

RICK VENTURI
Northwestern football coach, after his team suffered a 43-point loss to Ohio State:

"The only difference between me and General Custer is that I had to watch the films on Sunday."

LOU HOLTZ
Arkansas football coach, opening his weekly television show after his team suffered its fourth loss in five weeks:

"Welcome to the Lou Holtz Show. Unfortunately, I'm Lou Holtz."

DAVE BRISTOL
San Francisco Giants manager, addressing his team after a loss:

"There'll be two buses leaving the hotel for the park tomorrow. The 2 o'clock bus will be for those of you who need a little extra work. The empty bus will leave at 5 o'clock."

BILL BRADLEY
U.S. senator and former New York Knicks forward:

"The taste of defeat has a richness of experience all its own."

DR. THOMAS TUTKO
sports psychologist:

"Winning is like drinking salt water; it will never quench your thirst. It is an insatiable greed."

AL MCGUIRE
sportscaster, recalling his days as a college basketball coach:

"When I was losing, they called me nuts. When I was winning, they called me eccentric."

JOHN R. TUNIS
writer, in the early thirties:

"We [Americans] worship the victors. But why? The Dutch don't especially, nor the Swedes; neither do the Danes, the Swiss, or the English, and they all seem fairly civilized people."

GEORGE ALLEN
professional football coach:

"The man who can accept defeat and take his salary without feeling guilty is a thief."

ARMAND "BEP" GUIDOLIN
former Boston Bruins coach:

"Winning is the name of the game. The more you win the less you get fired."

BOB DEVANEY
Nebraska football coach, upon being hired:

"I don't expect to win enough games to be put on NCAA probation. I just want to win enough to warrant an investigation."

BILL COSBY
comedian, recalling the hapless football team he played on at Temple University:

"We lost every week. We lost to schools I never heard of. I think guys used to get together and invent a name just so they could play us. One year we lost to a school called 'We Want U.'"

WALT MCALEXANDER
Lubbock Christian College sports publicist, explaining the firing of football coach Jerry Don Sanders, who had won just once in two years:

"The athletic council said it could only take so many of these great lessons in humility."

KNUTE ROCKNE
Notre Dame football coach:

"One loss is good for the soul. Too many losses are not good for the coach."

DANNY WHELAN
New York Knicks trainer:

"When you lose the *must* game, it wasn't a must game."

EARL MONROE
professional basketball player:

"If you lose the must game, the next one is a *really* must game."

RED HOLZMAN
New York Knicks coach:

"When you lose the must game, the *next* one becomes a must game."

ROBERT REDFORD
actor:

"I inherited a false legacy about sports. I was told it wasn't whether you won or lost, but how you played the game. I found out that was nonsense. It *is* who wins, and nobody remembers who finishes second. In this country, we'll tolerate winners and their behavior—the Connorses, the Nastases, the Alis. It almost seems fashionable to be an ass, to be out of control and undisciplined and have only the ability to win. I believe we tolerate that because we like winners."

MIKE REID
Cincinnati Bengals defensive lineman:

"The most intangible aspect of winning and losing is the human heart."

JOHN ROBINSON
University of Southern California football coach:

"People have the perception that you are a winner or a loser. There's no such thing; all of us have a little loser in us."

WOODY HAYES
Ohio State football coach:

"Winners are men who have dedicated their whole lives to winning."

DIGGER PHELPS
Notre Dame basketball coach, asked by Irish alumnus Carl Yastrzemski when his team was finally going to win a championship:

"Funny, I was about to ask you the same question."

JOHN MCKAY
Tampa Bay Buccaneers coach, asked following a loss to Cleveland what he thought of his team's execution:

"I think it's a good idea."

BEAR BRYANT
Alabama football coach:

"A tie is like kissing your sister."

EDDIS FREEMAN
South Carolina high school football coach, asked if a complicated new strategy would win for his team:

"No, but it's one with which we can lose with dignity."

DARRELL HEDRICK
Miami of Ohio basketball coach, after a loss to Purdue:

"If you want to know the turning point, it was our lay-up drill."

CHARLIE CONERLY
former New York Giants quarterback:

"When you win, you're an old pro. When you lose, you're an old man."

DUFFY DAUGHERTY
Michigan State football coach:

"When you're playing for the national championship, it's not a matter of life or death. It's more important than that."
   (Also attributed to UCLA football coach Red Sanders in reference to the UCLA–USC rivalry)

PETER GENT
professional football player-turned-writer:

"Winning is a matter of opinion. But losing is a cold reality."

CHRIS EVERT LLOYD
professional tennis player:

"Losses are always a relief. They take a great burden off me, make me feel more normal. If I win several tournaments in a row I get so confident I'm in a cloud. A loss gets me eager again."

JOHN R. TUNIS
writer:

"There's such a thin line between winning and losing. Yet the laurels only go to the winner. The rush is always to the champion."

LOU HOLTZ
Arkansas football coach:

"There's only one bright side of losing—the phone doesn't ring as much the following week."

WOODY HAYES
Ohio State football coach:

"Winning is still the most honorable thing a man can do."

JOE LOUIS
former heavyweight boxing champion:

"Every man's got to figure to get beat sometime."

LAVELL EDWARDS
Brigham Young University football coach, on why he likes Sherlock Holmes:

"I love those guys who win 'em all."

MARK FIDRYCH
major league pitcher:

"When you're a winner you're always happy, but if you're happy as a loser you'll always be a loser."

WOODY HAYES
Ohio State football coach:

"There's nothing in this world that comes easy. There are a lot of people who aren't going to bother to win. We learn in football to get up and go once more."

DARRELL ROYAL
Texas football coach:

"The only way I know how to keep football fun is to win. That's the only answer. There is no laughter in losing."

DON NELSON
Milwaukee Bucks coach, after a sloppily played victory:

"We don't care how the grapes were crushed as long as the wine turns out fine."

BILLIE JEAN KING
professional tennis player:

"A champion is afraid of losing. Everyone else is afraid of winning."

BEAR BRYANT
Alabama football coach, asked what he most wanted to be remembered for:

"I'd like if it'd be for winning. . . . That's our approach: if it's worth playing, it's worth paying the price to win."

WOODY HAYES
Ohio State football coach:

"There's nothing that cleanses your soul like getting the hell kicked out of you."

GEORGE STEINBRENNER
New York Yankees owner:

"I want this team to win. I'm obsessed with winning, with discipline, with achieving. That's what this country's all about, that's what New York is all about—fighting for everything: a cab in the rain, a table in a restaurant at lunchtime. And that's what the Yankees are all about and always have been."

TOM SEAVER
New York Mets pitcher:

"There are only two places in this league: first place and no place."

JOHN MCGRAW
New York Giants manager:

"In playing or managing, the game of ball is only fun for me when I'm out in front and winning. I don't care a bag of peanuts for the rest of the game."

JOHN MCKAY
University of Southern California football coach, to his team after a 51–0 loss to Notre Dame:

"All those who need showers, take them."

EMLEN TUNNELL
New York Giants Hall of Fame safety:

"Losers assemble in little groups to share their misery and to bitch about the coaches and the guys in other little groups. Winners assemble as a team."

JOHNNY PESKY
Boston Red Sox manager:

"When you win, you eat better, sleep better and your beer tastes better. And your wife looks like Gina Lollobrigida."

JIMMY BRYAN
sportswriter, reporting on a 66–3 Vanderbilt loss to Alabama:

"Inflation killed the Vanderbilt Commodores Saturday. Once the football was inflated, Vanderbilt was dead."

TOMMY PROTHRO
UCLA football coach:

"It isn't necessary to say that a football team loses. I prefer the language of the Olympics, in which you say somebody won second."

JOHN MCKAY
Tampa Bay Buccaneers coach, on the Pittsburgh Steelers:

"They have so many Super Bowl rings that maybe they'll retire and go into the jewelry business."

TED TURNER
Atlanta Braves and Hawks owner:

"It's not a disaster if we don't win. It's a game. The song says, 'If they don't win it's a shame.' It's a *shame*, not a disaster."

JIM MCKINLEY
North Carolina A & T football coach, on why he doesn't subscribe to the theory that underdog status has its advantages:

"Underdogs usually lose."

RED SANDERS
college football coach:

"The only thing worse than finishing second is to be lying on the desert alone with your back broke. Either way, nobody ever finds out about you."

DARRELL ROYAL
Texas football coach:

"The best thing a coach can hope for is to please the majority. And the only way to please the majority is to win."

BEAR BRYANT
Alabama football coach:

"If someone has to be the winningest coach, it might as well be me."

WOODY HAYES
Ohio State football coach:

"There are too damn many in school who don't know how to win."

DARRELL ROYAL
Texas football coach:

"There is no such thing as defeat except when it comes from within. As long as a person doesn't admit he is defeated, he is not defeated—he's just a little behind and isn't through fighting."

NEILL ARMSTRONG
Chicago Bears coach:

"Regardless of how you play for 59 minutes, all that counts in the end is winning."

TOM CAHILL
Army football coach:

"One thing I don't like about losing is the winkers. They don't know what to say to you, so they just wink when they see you."

PAUL BROWN
NFL coach and executive:

"A winner never whines."

HANK STRAM
Kansas City Chief's coach:

"It's only a game when you win. When you lose, it's hell."

DARRELL ROYAL
Texas football coach:

"The only place you can win a football game is on the field. The only place you can lose is in your hearts."

CHRISTY MATHEWSON
Hall of Fame pitcher:

"You can learn little from victory. You can learn everything from defeat."

A. BARTLETT GIAMATTI
Yale University president:

"Winning has a joy and discrete purity to it that cannot be replaced by anything else. Winning is important to any man's or woman's sense of satisfaction and well-being. Winning is not everything; but it is something powerful, indeed beautiful, in itself, something as necessary to the strong spirit as striving is necessary to the healthy character."

TIM FOLEY
Miami Dolphins safety:

"Humility is always one play away."

BUM PHILLIPS
New Orleans Saints coach, after viewing the game film of a lopsided loss to the Atlanta Falcons:

"The film looks suspiciously like the game itself."

Index

Copyright Acknowledgments